Memories of Madison County

Memories
of Madison
County

JANA ST. JAMES

with Richard Hack

DOVE
BOOKS

ISBN 0-7871-0657-7

Printed in the United States of America

Dove Books
301 North Cañon Drive
Beverly Hills, CA 90210

Distributed by Penguin USA

Text design and layout by Folio Graphics Co., Inc.
Photos courtesy of Richard Hack and Jana St. James

First Printing: October 1995

1 2 3 4 5 6 7 8 9 10

For Everyone Who Has Ever Had to Let Go of Love . . .

CONTENTS

ACKNOWLEDGMENTS

It is with respect and admiration that I express my appreciation to Michael Viner and Richard Hack. I salute them, as well as the entire staff at Dove, for their encouragement, guidance, and patience. And to my editor, Lee Montgomery, I raise accolades not only to her exceptional talent but also to her dedication to task. I am in her debt.

I am proud to have a very special group of friends who have believed in me through good times and bad. Thanks to Chris, Rolland, Gregg, Gayle and Jay, Haley, and Joanne for always being there. Additional encouragement came from a variety of people in and around the DDLA days and I will always be grateful for the special talents of Ron, David, and Con.

Finally, and most especially, I want to thank Stacey, who makes it all worthwhile.

The brain may take advice, but not the heart, and love, having no geography, knows no boundaries.

TRUMAN CAPOTE
Other Voices, Other Rooms

FOREWORD

Love can be a risky business, especially when it is a young love, one filled with innocent emotions and unexplored dreams. In 1967 Jana St. James had such a love. A fleeting, intense, passionate love with a married man ten years her senior, a man who has since gone on to become one of the nation's most celebrated writers following the publication of a little book called *The Bridges of Madison County*.

But long before Robert James Waller's success, before the three years on the *New York Times* bestseller list, before the appearances on "The Oprah Winfrey Show" and "Sunday Morning," before the CD of country ballads, before the movie, the music video, and three other books, Robert James Waller was Jana St. James's mentor, lover, and best friend.

In 1995, almost three decades later, my wife and partner, Deborah Raffin, and I had the good fortune of meeting Jana at a Los Angeles dinner party hosted by mutual friends at their beautiful beachfront home. It was a warm spring evening in April, a few years after the publication of *Bridges* and shortly after the film version was released. From the moment we met Jana, we were struck by her warmth and beauty, and not only did that impression grow stronger each moment we talked, but both Deborah and I also found her to be extraordinarily sensitive, genuine, and witty. In short, we were captivated by her, much like I imagine Waller must have been so many years ago.

At dinner the conversation was lively and moved quickly from politics to books to movies, and of course Waller as well as other famous names surfaced during the course of the meal. As Jana was seated next to me, and I was somewhat curious about her, it was difficult not to notice a dramatic change in her face when Waller's name first came up. While many were quite enthusiastic about the man and his work, Jana seemed suddenly uncomfortable, troubled, and the change was so noticeable I couldn't help but ask her about it later when we were all taking a stroll on the beach.

It was a lovely evening as the mist crawled

toward the shore from the sea. Jana was walking a few steps behind the others, quiet, seemingly lost in her thoughts. Deborah and I slowed up to keep even with her pace.

"So I gather you weren't that impressed with Mr. Waller's work," Deborah said.

"Oh, no, I love it," she said hesitantly.

"Then why did you seem so uncomfortable at dinner?" I asked.

"Brings back my own memories, I guess," she replied. "I knew Bob. Actually, quite well once."

"Who?"

"Bob Waller."

"The author?" I asked.

She stopped and looked at me and Deborah, her large blue eyes smiling. "Yes," she whispered. "The author. But when I knew him, he wasn't *the* Robert Waller. He was a student, a musician, a friend."

As we walked on, we fell farther behind the others and after a time Jana began speaking about more than just a friendship of long ago. She told us of a love affair with a man who had obviously made a strong, lasting impression on her, and both Deborah and I could sense that despite the time, despite the distance, Jana was still feeling the sadness of her loss. Over the course of the next several hours, that loss grew as Jana gradually revealed a story about a young girl's love affair with a married man that shared so many parallels to the story of Robert Kincaid and Francesca Johnson, I knew it had to be more than a coincidence.

It took some time, but after several months I finally managed to talk Jana St. James into writing the real story behind lost loves in the Midwest. It is a powerful story of a young woman who loses her heart, yet despite her strong feelings is able to walk away from a man she deeply loved. It is an impassioned story about first love—real love—and as you'll see, this time Madison County is more than just a location in Iowa. It is a state of mind, a special place that exists in the form of memories for all of us who have deeply loved and have had to let go.

September 1995
Michael Viner, Publisher
Dove Books
Beverly Hills, California

ONE

Quiet Rooms

It tears me up inside to think of you now
Walking the streets of some other town
On your way this very afternoon
To spend a little time
In some other quiet room.

January 20, 1992
Los Angeles, California

T he black waters of the Pacific had gained strength from the storm, pitching and churning in majestic white caps before crashing on the shore. It was the time of year Southern Californians hated, when the beaches that had given birth to L.A.'s legendary lifestyle were shunned as if they were traitors. Christmas 1991 now seemed long gone, 1992 had been welcomed in, and the endless stretch of days until springtime loomed before me, gray and chilly, with frequent rain showers tossed into the mix.

The weather didn't help the sagging spirits around the advertising office that drizzly Friday afternoon in January, where last-minute broadcast time was being bought up left and right, whipping us all into a frenzy to beat a variety of deadlines. The stress level and weather conditions were annual occurrences, but while adjustments could be made for the stress, bad weather was always intolerable, especially for those raised in Southern California. In protest, the natives struck giant black crosses through the passing days on their calendars in a kind of ritualistic vigil as they impatiently awaited another long, perfect summer season. In these surroundings, I never dared mention how much I liked this weather, how it always brought back memories of growing up in the Midwest, and though many of them were pleasant, I had long since learned that certain memories always look better from far away.

By the end of the day, I was ready to go home and enjoy a relaxing weekend. The weather, unfortunately, had no respect for my state of mind. Westbound traffic on the Ventura Freeway was backed up at the Hollywood Freeway split due to the rain, forcing me to ride my clutch through the four-and-a-half-mile gauntlet to the San Diego Freeway interchange. At that junction, hundreds of cars bound for West Los Angeles and points south would peel off and relieve the snarl on the Ventura, allowing me to utilize my accelerator again. It took a total of an hour and a half to cover twenty-five miles and, by the time I finally reached home, I wanted nothing more than to get inside quickly and shut the door.

Concentrating on fitting the key into the lock, I almost overlooked a small note strategically stuck over the peephole in my front door. Not until I had kicked off my shoes, removed my coat, and turned on the bright light in the kitchen did I glance down at the note I had inadvertently crumpled in my haste to remove it from the door. I smoothed it out on the countertop, turned to the refrigerator to retrieve a pitcher of iced tea, took a glass from the cabinet, and had already finished pouring before my eyes finally took in the words that informed me a package had been left on my patio deck. A late Christmas gift, maybe? My spirits lifted. I quickly crossed through the dining area of my small condominium and opened the sliding glass door. A brown envelope, bulging in the middle, sat neatly tucked under the doormat.

I smiled as I slid the door shut and snapped the lock, and seeing the return address on the package as Cedar Falls, Iowa, I knew it was from Robert Waller. Although we hadn't seen each other in years, we had been corresponding annually for the last six or seven. Because I moved often, it had become customary for me to write first. About a month earlier, I'd enclosed a letter with the Christmas card I sent to him. I wasn't surprised to see the package; he often sent things along with his letters that would give me a better idea of what he'd been doing. One year I received several newspaper clippings of articles written by and about him in the *Des Moines Register*; another year it was a cassette tape by Winter Ridge Handy, his musical group. In more recent years he'd sent two books of his essays published by the Iowa State University Press. On the title page of the first book, *Just Beyond the Firelight*, he'd written "For Jana & all the old winds" above his autograph. I was anxious to see what new treasure this package held.

After carefully opening the envelope, I extracted a letter and a copy of his new book, *The Bridges of Madison County*. I remembered his mentioning it the year before and was delighted to see it in finished form. But I set it aside for the moment to read the latest news in his letter about his writing efforts and travels. I was disappointed to learn he'd been trucking around the Southwest and had entered California but turned back. "I was driven back by dust storms, hard rain, and the incredible intensity I find there," he wrote. In an earlier letter, back in 1988, he had said, "Go well, my friend. If I come your way sometime, I'll call. Meanwhile, take care of yourself and your life. I remember you."

It had been a quarter of a century since I'd last seen him and, although we'd fantasized about it when we parted years ago, it seemed more and more unlikely we would ever meet again. My attention was drawn to the new book as he explained in his last paragraph that what he was sending me was one of his complimentary copies from the publisher. As it would not be in stores until April, he asked me to keep my copy to myself but spread the word if I liked it. He wrote:

My protagonist, one Robert Kincaid, is one of the last pure men, understands his masculinity, and is not afraid of it. Calls himself "the last cowboy." A woman in the book says he exists "in logic." I loved him as a character, loved her just as much. Loved them so much I never wanted the book to end. At one point, I simply stopped and cried at the beauty of their feelings for one another, then returned to the keyboard with a towel around my neck so I could wipe my eyes as I wrote.

I folded the letter and placed it carefully inside the cover of the book, which I picked up and began examining. Again he had personalized the autograph on the title page, this time dating it to show I had received it prior to official publication. I decided to change into comfortable clothes and grab something to eat before getting further into the book, so I took it into my bedroom and laid it gently on the pillow. I had no idea that within its pages, underneath fictitious characters, unfamiliar locations, and transposed circumstances, the premise for the book was the very real emotional anguish Robert and I had suffered when we chose to part so long ago. Less than an hour later, when I settled down to read, I was totally unprepared for the effect the book would have on me.

As the story unfolded, so did the memories I'd struggled so long to repress. I spun backward in time, feeling the sadness from that period with him, a sadness twenty-five years old yet suddenly as fresh as yesterday. He was my first love, my most intense and dear love, and as I read I felt a tingling sensation spread through my arms, and my hands began to shake. Later in the book, when I read his description of how his heroine could hardly bear remembering the love of her life "or her mind somehow would have disintegrated at the sheer emotional bludgeoning of it all," I leaned my head back and closed my reddened eyes. *If he were insightful enough to write those words,* I wondered, *why would he do this to me?*

I sat up and swung my legs over the edge of the bed, needing a moment of relief from the intensity of my feelings as I struggled to understand. Ours was a story I had always protected, hurting and forsaking people who had cared about me and sometimes imperiling myself, and there it sat in black and white. I knew it would be torture to continue reading, but I couldn't resist, just as I had been unable to resist him all those years ago.

The characters in the book chose to separate for the same reasons Bob and I had. In the letter sent from his hero to the woman he loved saying how leaving the relationship had been "the hardest thing I've ever done or will ever do," I was haunted by the memory of the same words he'd written to me after we'd parted in the summer of 1967. I continued to read, seeing parallel after parallel, and when I finally finished the last page I leaned back on the bed and closed my eyes. Emotional exhaustion carried me into a state somewhere between sleep and wakefulness. The image of Bob as I knew him years ago drifted in and out of my consciousness and, when morning came, his visit seemed so real I looked around the room to see if he was there.

Later that morning I drove out to Malibu to give myself some time to think. The ocean seemed glad to have a visitor, putting extra effort into its performance as the waves raised up high and proud before crashing at my feet. For hours I walked, alone, down the foggy, desolate beach, reliving my days with Robert. There were no tears; the feelings were buried so deep down in-side they could not surface. Finally the sym-phony of the sea calmed me enough to allow the thinking process to begin. In all our years of corresponding, I had never once told him how our relationship had affected my life. I had al-ways tried to stay strong for him and wanted to continue to do so.

Because his book felt so personal to me, I mentioned it only to a few of my closest friends and then placed it up on a shelf alongside his collections of essays. I was hoping to forget it, and for nearly a year I did manage to block it out along with the remembrances it had brought back so vividly. But it kept coming back to me at odd moments—as I was driving, before bed—and soon I had to face the fact that I could no longer get away from it. I struggled instead to try to understand why, after all this time, it was still so difficult to deal with these memories.

In March of 1993, I saw Robert for the first time in twenty-six years when he was interviewed on the "Sunday Morning" television show on CBS. Although my mind knew that time had passed, my heart still saw a young man and I was surprised to see his hair had turned to gray and lines had formed in his gentle face. It warmed my heart to see that his smile was still the same. In May he was a guest on "The Oprah Winfrey Show," and I listened carefully when she asked him who his heroine was based on. He explained she was "a composite" and told Oprah he had written the book only for himself. Was there a message there for me?

As the popularity of Robert's book grew, so did the publicity, and my difficulties increased. He had taken the world by storm and, although I was touched by reports of the heartfelt emotion it was generating, I was annoyed with the debate over the outcome of the story. I was amazed at the number of people who were focusing only on the surface love that exists during affairs when in fact I knew that true love exists in the ability to let go. In an era when relationships between men and women seem to be more about tearing apart than building up, when sex has become a substitute for love, when possessing a person is preferable to freeing a soul, I finally made up my mind that it was time to lay down the true story. I wrote a long letter to Robert but, because he had moved and left no forwarding address, the letter remains undelivered.

I met Bob Waller in 1967, the year I left my family and home in northwest Indiana to head south to the college town of Bloomington, where I was to attend Indiana University. Lyndon B. Johnson was president of the United States, the country was in the midst of the turbulent sixties, in January the Apollo astronauts met with disaster, and college campuses around the nation were exploding with diverse new music—acid rock versus folk ballads. I had just turned eighteen and was beginning the arduous journey of my life as a woman and an adult when suddenly, unexpectedly, I fell in love.

TWO

Red Velvet

Four months ago in April
On a day coach she came down,
And the dusty autumn winds
Began to blow . . .

Late January 1967
Bloomington, Indiana

Winter sliced through Bloomington with a deliberate strength that did more than merely blanket the streets and limestone quarries with snowdrifts four feet high. The air cut into skin like ice as the temperature dropped to seventeen degrees above zero. In what was surely a test of man versus nature, nature was winning—and winning big.

After dinner one Friday evening, I stared out

my dorm room window at the hushed campus of Indiana University. The glass panes were damp with condensation as I lay on my bed absently watching huddled figures in the distance rush quickly past one another through the cold. Even under deep-freeze conditions, the campus was still undeniably beautiful.

It was late January and school was closed for semester break. I was one of a dozen or so girls stranded by the weather on the fifth floor of Read Center, our dormitory. It had been a week of forced camaraderie for a group of women who had little in common. Under normal circumstances, we would have continued to pass in hallways without acknowledging one another's presence. Out of necessity, though, we had warmed to one another and amused ourselves with small talk, card games, and long-playing records. I'd even pulled out my guitar on several occasions and invited them to sing along. But now we felt trapped, like a band of captives, imprisoned by the cold and weary of its relentless onslaught.

I had moved beyond boredom. Everything was shut down; there was absolutely nothing to do. I thought about my friends who had managed to escape for break and felt envious. Some were off enjoying the warmth of Fort Lauderdale, others were home on laundry runs. As much as I would have liked to spend the break away from school, I couldn't afford a trip to Florida and the weather conditions made going home too risky.

I had paid a visit home a month earlier, returning to Munster in northwest Indiana to celebrate the Christmas holidays with my family. The festivities were great; the weather that followed wasn't. Blizzard conditions set in and showed no signs of letting up. The days passed slowly as I fought the restlessness that pulled at me, body and soul. I felt I had outgrown my place in the family and was eager to return to the independence university life offered. As firm advocates of higher education, my parents were equally anxious for me to get back on time.

We may have been at cross purposes, but we shared the same mission when the appointed day arrived and we set out to challenge the harshest of winter conditions to get me back to the university. Despite the overtime put in by the snowplow crews, only a few roads remained passable, and even those were too icy to negotiate safely. The train remained the only alternative, if unpredictable, form of transportation. Regular schedules were being canceled or altered with the movement of storms, and the few runs that were being attempted could change in the time it took to get from home to the station.

Undaunted, my parents and I set out, refusing to be intimidated by the inherent danger on the roads, my father inching our station wagon across the ten miles that separated our house from the local train station. Midway through our trek, a new storm blew in from the north, making the road as invisible as the oncoming traffic. Headlamps became phantoms of unconnected lights, swaying in unison as tires skidded across ice. In moments my parents and I changed from travelers into explorers, forsaking logic and reason as we charted new territory on once familiar ground.

Arriving at the station, I discovered that yet another adventure lay ahead. To get from the car to the train, I had to cross an obstacle course of nine-foot piles of packed snow in a frozen canyon that used to be a parking lot. Sliding at last onto the boarding platform, I swung myself onto the 10:18 southbound to Bloomington just as it pulled out of the station. As the train began its journey across the frigid landscape, I waved a hearty good-bye to my parents, eager to return to my newfound freedom on the college campus.

The memory of that struggle reminded me why I had decided to stay at school during the semester break. Still, as I lay on my bed with nothing to do on that cold Friday night, it occurred to me that common sense was a poor substitute for the exciting possibilities I'd had in mind a couple of weeks ago on that train ride back to school. I had thought I was ready for anything. Only time would prove how wrong I was.

I sighed, pushed myself up from the bed, and silently began to draw patterns in the condensation on the dormitory windows. Hearts, circles, and boxes. A picture of the sun and musical notes. The more I drew, the clearer my reflection became, silhouetted as it was against the frost and snow outside. Instinctively, my hand moved to my hair. A pause, a tug, then another sigh passed my lips, exposing my uncertainty at the new short-cropped Twiggy cut I had adopted in place of the long, thick hair that had been my trademark in high school. The waiflike supermodel had set the fashion trend for thousands of young women around the world, and I was no exception. Fortunately, the style suited my small features. I tugged my hair again and watched my eyes and face light up in a resigned smile as I fell back down on the bed. Lying there with my back now facing the window, I had an excellent view of my closet, where I could see clothes jammed and bunched into the top shelf. Straightening this out was not a very exciting prospect, but neither was sleep, glaring through the window, or playing cards. I reluctantly dragged my desk chair over to the closet edge, took off my jeans for comfort, and dug in, throwing half my wardrobe to the floor.

I had been perched there on my tiptoes for nearly half an hour when three of my stranded acquaintances suddenly burst into the room. Startled, I grabbed for the wall, pulling one knee up for balance. They giggled at the sight of me, dressed in a huge sweatshirt with a hint of panties peeking out from underneath, and commented that I looked remarkably like a flamingo in this bizarre position. I relaxed and adjusted my balance so I could lower my arms and laughed along with them. The oldest girl, Jane, was the first to recover and get to the point of their visit. They had discovered the Kiva was open and it was time to get out and have some fun.

"You've got to come," she said. "It'll be a blast."

"Brrrr . . ." I said, pointing to the frosted canvas of my window.

The Kiva was a sometime campus coffee-house in the basement of the Student Union cafeteria. It had been hastily created by the student activities committee of the university to accommodate the influx of folk music enthusiasts. Knowing firsthand of my love for this music, the girls had kindly thought to include me in their plans. The idea sounded good, but there was no escaping the fact that my room was a total nightmare. Glancing down at the heap of clothes around me, I felt a momentary responsibility to stay behind and finish my newly appointed task.

"You guys," I said hesitantly, "I really appreciate your asking me, but I've got all this stuff to fold and put away before my roommate gets back on Sunday and besides, the snow is three feet deep and it's bitter cold outside and . . ."

They looked at me, eyes wide and mouths agape, as if they were saying, "Have you lost your mind?" *Oh, what the heck,* I thought. *I'll get this done tomorrow.* Needing no further encouragement, I jumped to the floor, leaving the chair to topple sideways into the clothes pile behind me. Delighted with my return to sanity, the girls cheered and scattered off to find warm clothes.

"Meet us at the elevator in fifteen minutes," they shouted over their shoulders.

As I pulled my jeans back on, I spotted a sweater buried among the clothes on the floor that had a nice, high collar to cover my naked neck and quickly set about dressing. I put on some pale lipstick and a little mascara, then dashed down the hall to join the group at the elevator.

We spilled into the empty lobby on the ground floor, threw open the front door, and were promptly swept back in by a fierce, icy wind.

"See?" I taunted. "I told you. Cold. C-O-L—" They turned in unison, raising their hands in a mock gesture as if they were going to strangle me. I took off running around the lobby, teasing and laughing as they gave chase. This time we hit the door like four falling dominoes and beat back the wind. Fortunately the concrete steps had been dusted with rock salt, or we might have slipped and ended up in a heap of broken bones. Instead, we went laughing into the weather, pressing forward against the mean gusts and carefully negotiating the slick side-walk that wound along the downhill drive to Jordan Avenue. Boot-skating to the street, we considered taking the sensible path down Jordan to Seventh, which had recently been plowed, but opted instead to take the scenic route through the woods.

Bounding across Jordan, we were immediately forced to an abrupt halt in front of the Delta Gamma house. The three-story, red-brick sorority was the newest house in this older section of the campus and had been positioned perpendicular to the street to allow for a vast, rolling lawn, now covered with snow. We slid forward cautiously, unaided by the streetlamps that tonight served only to create sparkling illusions in the endless blanket of white. We had to feel for the sidewalk we knew lay buried along the base of the lawn and followed it into one of the many wooded areas that distinguish the university's original site. Now a dark charcoal gray in the moonlight, the woods were almost eerie with black, brittle branches dueling overhead, struggling futilely to touch the stars. Our boots were soaked and, feeling as though ice cubes had formed below our ankles, we skidded across a little pedestrian bridge over a frozen brook where cardinals would bathe in the springtime. All conversation ended at that point, due largely to the numbness spreading through our uncovered faces. With red noses, brittle chins, and frostbite threatening our toes, we came out of the woods alongside a revered campus landmark known as Beck Chapel.

As quickly as our frozen feet would carry us, we slipped and stumbled across the uneven sheet of ice covering the plowed parking lot in front of the majestic Student Union building. This massive alabaster structure shone brightly in the moonlight, a testimony to the beauty of celebrated Indiana limestone. Although students may not have fully appreciated the splendor and value of the stone, they certainly enjoyed swimming in the rain-filled quarries that provided it. Standing in the center of the old campus, the Student Union was virtually a mini-metropolis, boasting such amenities as hotel rooms, meeting rooms, restaurants, hair salons, a student cafeteria, bookstores, and even a game room with full-size pool tables.

After we stomped the snow off our boots, it took two of us on either side to pull open the Union's heavy double doors. We were rewarded for our efforts by a welcoming hug of heat. Leaving puddles of melting snow behind us, we made our way through a maze of hallways to the now empty cafeteria. Chairs enough to seat at least 250 were upended on tabletops while floors were being mopped. A couple of kitchen workers were unceremoniously banging freshly washed pans into cupboards. Faces now thawed by the building's warmth, the other three girls were all talking at once, smoothing their damp hair and excitedly working their way toward the open staircase that led from the cafeteria to the Kiva below.

Suddenly the cacophony of sound became a distant hum to me; the brightly lit cafeteria grew dim. The girls faded to vague shapes around me. My stride broke and I felt like I was suddenly moving in—what was it? Slow motion? I felt enveloped by a sensation I had never felt before. The air seemed electric, charged with energy, drawing me into its mysterious power.

At first I felt more than heard the faint sound of his gentle song. It drifted up the open staircase and across the room, echoing in my mind and enveloping my senses while tying itself in a loose knot around my unsuspecting heart. Softly it came to rest in a corner of my soul, where it would delicately but firmly influence my life for years to come.

Moving slowly with the shadows of the others, I approached the L-shaped staircase, edging closer to the source of the captivating sound. The first set of steps led to a landing where a small table served as an admission booth for the coffeehouse. Because my back was facing the stage at this point, I didn't notice the performer staring at me as I fumbled for a quarter to pay the entrance fee. After a moment, though, acoustic guitar mixed with gentle voice urged me to glance in his direction and I found him looking straight at me. So powerful was the combination of his music and his eyes, I turned away, but not out of a sense of fear. No, it wasn't that. I was far too young, too inexperienced to be drawing on the subconscious warning signals that guide us through such things as we grow older.

I remember focusing my eyes on the dimly lit room as I descended the second set of steps, catching the scent of stale tobacco and the haze of smoke drifting from countless ashtrays on a number of intimately arranged small tables. Covered with quaint squares of red-and-white gingham, each table was surrounded by old-fashioned wooden chairs that lent an Italian bistro atmosphere to an otherwise dismal place. Candles glowed inside red glass globes, creating centerpieces that cast imperfect shadows on fresh faces, with eyes reflecting untarnished dreams.

Crunching through the layer of peanut shells that littered the floor, my pals selected a table to the left of the stage. Once we were settled in our seats, we ordered drinks from the waitress in hushed tones. Finally we sat back and began to listen. Only then was I able to take a deep breath and slowly raise my eyes to meet his. He was still staring into me, and though I tried to look away from him, to avert his curious gaze, I couldn't. It hadn't been a matter of catching each other's eyes. There was no adjusting, no focusing necessary. He had been watching me since I arrived, patiently waiting and understanding, studying my movement, knowing my mind before he knew my name.

I sat transfixed, absorbing every note he sang as my eyes slowly took him in. He sat on a tall stool behind a microphone, bathed in the soft glow of a single spotlight, his guitar cradled in his strong arms. He wore a navy sweater and faded Levi's. His skin was fair in contrast to his dark, neatly trimmed hair and his face had a soft, kind, yet fully masculine quality. His pale blue eyes shaded when his song was sad and sparkled when the melody was light. His lips were soft and full and broke into a wide, generous smile when he looked at me. His long fingers curled around the guitar's neck and danced over the strings. His legs were long and the muscles of his thighs pressed against his jeans as his feet tapped out the rhythm. Beyond what I was recording with my eyes, there was something registering beyond the normal level of consciousness: a kind of recognition, a vague familiarity. It had been only an instant, yet I felt I had known and loved this man forever.

Lulled by his gentle vibrato, I began reflecting on the mystery of these feelings. I was not the type of person who just "fell in love" and though I was admittedly young and inexperienced, the rush of feelings spreading through my body was entirely new to me. What was even stranger was that I didn't even have to see him before I felt something move inside me. What was it? A quality in his voice? And what was this hesitation? A combination of fear and curiosity? What haunted me about his song? *Too many questions, Jana*, I thought to myself. *Don't give in to this.* Move closer to the other girls, join their conversation, anything to pull away. Suddenly the sound of applause interrupted my reverie. I joined in, clapping my hands softly as the singer smiled, first at me, and then to the rest of the room. With guitar in hand, he slowly unwound himself from the gray metal stool to stand before us. Now towering over the thin, pencil-style microphone, he had to bend down to meet it.

"Thank you," he spoke softly, in sensuous

31

tones. "Thank you very much. I'm going to take a short break and I'll be back in just a few minutes."

Again the room erupted with applause. As he left the stage, I continued staring at the empty stool, noticing for the first time that large speakers flanked it from behind, connected by a series of wires to the microphone. I kept my eyes on the reflection of the spotlight on the dirty plaster of the stage's back wall as if expecting him to magically reappear from within its glow. Someone tapped my shoulder, bringing me out of my daze, and I turned back to the table. I was surprised to find a mug of coffee in front of me. I hadn't realized the waitress had come and gone. My friends were already deeply engaged in girl talk; something about the cute guys sitting a few tables away. I kept trying to pay attention to them, but that lyrical voice was still echoing in my head when slowly, like bathwater, a sensation of warmth spread through me, across my back, past my cheek. Close. Touching. A hard, firm masculine arm touching my own. Turning, I saw his eyes moving to follow mine, his lips soft and full, separating in a generous smile.

The handsome singer had materialized beside me, just like that. He stared a second longer than was necessary for polite acknowledgment before turning his attention to the waitress and ordering coffee as he sat down at the next table. I smiled briefly before turning away. But my curiosity and excitement got the better of me, and a moment later I glanced back and saw him light a cigarette. After avoiding him so carefully at first, I now found I couldn't stop looking at him. He must have felt my eyes, for he turned to me and, hesitantly, our first conversation began.

"Hello," he said. "What brings you out on such a cold evening?" He smiled and sipped at his coffee.

"Oh, ah, madness, maybe?" I stammered. I could barely speak, I was so overwhelmed with feelings for this man. "I mean, you have to be crazy to go out in weather like this, right?"

Up until this moment, we had enjoyed the ease of communicating through a kind of telepathy. Now words were called for and we weren't sure what to say next. I was afraid to give it a try and the sensation did not disappear as his eyes crept toward mine again and again. Each time he looked at me, our eyes would become

33

locked momentarily and when I found the courage to peer deeply into their pale blue warmth, I felt like I was falling into him and he into me.

"Your music is wonderful," I finally offered, looking away with uncustomary shyness. Something was happening between us and I felt totally vulnerable. *Fight it, Jana, fight it.* Struggling to keep my distance, I spoke into the candle, "I really enjoyed your singing."

He leaned over and placed his face close enough to recapture my gaze again.

"Thank you," he said with a smile.

"Your fingering on the Irish ballad was incredible," I said, smiling back.

"Do you play?" he asked, adjusting his long legs and leaning closer still.

"A little," I said. "In fact, a few months ago I played here."

"Really?" he said. "I'm sorry I missed it."

"I'm not," I laughed.

I was actually happy we hadn't met that way. My simple strumming lacked his skill, and I told him as much.

"It's actually quite simple—logical, in fact," he remarked. "It just takes practice."

Guitar technique provided a safe and comfortable subject for us to talk about while our eyes continued to carry on a silent conversation all their own.

After some time, he glanced at his watch, then nodded toward the stage. "Showtime," he said, as he stood up and moved to the spotlight. Reality snapped back into place for me, as I fought to hold on to the last fading tendrils of certainly the most captivating "intermission" I could remember.

The audience greeted his reemergence with cheers of appreciation as his voice cut through the smoke and white noise of idle chatter once again.

"This is one of my favorites," he announced. "A little Ian and Sylvia tune called 'Red Velvet.' "

He began to sing.

Four months ago in April
On a day coach she came down,
And the dusty autumn winds began to blow . . .

Occasionally he would look in my direction, smiling and filling my stomach with that crazy anticipatory feeling that happens just as a roller coaster completes its first climb.

If I'd only known
Before we kissed—
You can't keep Red Velvet on a poor dirt farm like
  this . . .

He sang of love disappointed and love remembered. Strange, bittersweet lyrics aimed for the heart and hit their mark. I tried to remember the lines, an impossible task given the surrounding noise and my own state of mind. Instead, I concentrated on the muscles in his forearm as they flexed in rhythm with his string work. As I sat spellbound, a part of me longed to listen to him sing all night, yet another part of me wanted him to take another break so I could feel his warmth beside me again.

When he finally finished his second set, it seemed both too soon and too late. My emotions were ebbing and flowing in several directions at once. Returning to his seat next to me, there were more compliments, some additional talk about guitar technique, and even an offer from him to show me some basic picking patterns.

"I would love that," I said.

"Ready?" my girlfriends called out to me. I tried to ignore them.

"Jana. Ready? Let's go!" They were standing up, pointing to their watches and nodding toward the exit.

I smiled at him with a look of resignation and shrugged, hoping to communicate "curfew" through our newfound telepathy.

He nodded his understanding before hurriedly pulling a pen from his pocket and scratching his name and number on a paper napkin.

"Give me a call tomorrow," he said, handing me the napkin.

"Robert Waller," I read aloud before folding the napkin into my pocket. I looked up and answered his smile. "My name is Jana."

THREE

When Jana Was Young

Restless was she
Like a willow she caressed the wind
And as crystal autumn mornings
Fade into dusty afternoons
She passed my way
And was gone again.

Love has a way of coming along when you least expect it.

Emerging from the Student Union, I again measured my steps with caution, but this time it had nothing to do with concern for the jagged ice beneath my feet. Instead, I felt certain that if I were not careful I would glide across the parking lot like an Olympic figure skater, leaping and spinning with a grace that defies gravity but comes so easily to a heart in love. The freezing fingers of the wind were no match for the inner heat that spread from the bottom of my stomach to the end of my fingertips, and the sharp bite of the cold was conquered by cheeks that blushed and glowed with dreams of fairy tales come true. Unwilling and unable to share my feelings with the other girls, I lagged behind the group.

"Will you come on, Jana?" Their words were chopped to pieces by the harsh gusts that carried them to my ears.

"Yeah! What're you doing? Waiting for that guitar player to finish and catch up with us?" taunted Jane as the rest of them laughed. Ice swords plunged into their throats, forcing an abrupt end to their teasing and they moved on ahead, justly subdued. Even Mother Nature was on my side.

We entered the woods and, as I lifted my eyes upward to say a silent thank-you to heaven, I noticed the bare branches of the trees were no longer stark and menacing but now seemed crocheted together to form a warm, lacy coverlet. The stars that were hidden earlier congregated in dazzling splendor, portraying my inner radiance. All my life I had dreamed of finding the kind of love that would take hold of me and carry me high above the banalities of life, giving me all I would ever want or need. The cloudy, disjointed vision that had danced through my sleep for years stood before me only minutes earlier in the form of Robert Waller. Love was six feet tall with long, strong legs, appreciating eyes, and a smile that reached in and stirred up my insides in some curious way I'd never even imagined.

Back inside the dorm, waiting for the elevator with a group of girls I barely knew, I plastered a good-natured smile on my face for the sake of appearance. I could not speak and neither could they. We were too cold and the cozy building had yet to reheat our vocal cords. The mechanical thump of the elevator followed by the screech of scraping metal doors filled the lobby. We got in silently and rode up to the fifth floor. We moved in various directions down the hall, toward our respective rooms.

"Thanks for the good time," I called to them. "Thanks for asking me along." Jane wanted to say something. I could see thoughts forming but quickly cut her off with a "See ya later" as I walked into my room.

With the door closed tightly behind me, I wrapped my arms around myself and spun in circles across the room. No story I had ever read, no movie Hollywood had ever made, no dream I had ever dreamed had prepared me for the intensity of the feelings that filled my heart at that moment.

"This is what life is all about," I told the desks, the dresser, the closet doors. Tossing my coat onto the heap of unfolded clothes in the middle of the floor, I took the napkin from my pocket and held it close to my heart. What was happening to me? Who was this gentle stranger who had pulled me into his life? These were questions I could not answer. But I knew I would get to know this man named Robert. I carefully tucked the napkin under my bed pillow, and then, crossing the room, I turned off the light and waited for my eyes to adjust to the darkness.

I undressed slowly, leaving a trail of clothes behind me as I made my way toward the bed. I slipped my naked body between the cold sheets. I had never slept in the nude before and had no explanation for why I was doing it tonight. It just felt right. I reached for a cigarette, the flame of the lighter briefly intense, and then laid back against my pillow. Smiling in the dark,

I thought of his eyes flashing with recognition as he looked at me the first time. Again, I watched his lips part slowly, purposefully, and wondered how it would feel to touch them, kiss them, kiss him. Tenderly. Deeply. I put the cigarette to my lips and drew in my breath as though it were his spirit, exhaling it along with my own, giving it all back to him.

That's what love is about, I thought. Giving and taking. I turned on my side and slid my other hand under the pillow. The rough texture of the napkin met my fingers. I fell asleep touching its edge, and dreamed of having this man close to me. Of caring for him in good times and bad, of dedicating myself to his well-being, of growing old and gray beside him, of never faltering in my love. Of sharing his world and introducing him to mine. Of creating our own world together, wherever and whatever it might turn out to be.

The following morning I woke up slowly. As I lay in bed, studying the patterns in the white ceiling above me, the memory of the previous night began surfacing in visions and sounds. Robert Waller, the sound of his voice, his smile, and the indelible image of his body swaying to the beat of his music began circling through my mind over and over, again and again.

I wanted to call him, to hear his voice again. After breakfast I went to the phone several times, picking up the receiver, fingers shaking, but hesitating. Each time I put the phone down and told myself to relax. I didn't want to appear too anxious so I made an effort to finish folding the clothes I had thrown out of my closet the night before as my mind went back and forth about calling. I used every excuse I could imagine to keep from picking up the phone until early afternoon, when I decided the timing was right. I picked up the napkin and dialed the number.

On the third ring he answered, his voice strong and clear. He said he had been expecting my call. Robert Waller, the handsome stranger who sang love songs, had expected me to call. We talked a little about the night before and how it had gone after I left.

"I must have played until midnight," he said, "and by then, the place had pretty much cleared out."

"I really enjoyed your singing. I was so sorry I had to go," I said sadly, and meant it. "But, you know, curfew."

We talked a bit more and somehow got around to the subject of where we lived. As it turned out, he was in an apartment building directly behind Read Center. He said he'd been practicing when I called.

"Why don't you grab your guitar and come on over?" he asked. Just like that. No elaborate buildup, no playing for time.

"I'd love that," I responded while making a mental note of his apartment number.

After hanging up the phone, I went to my window and looked out over the rolling, snow-covered grassy area below, spotted with fine old trees and outlined by a series of sidewalks. Beyond this charming knoll were two four-story limestone buildings with brick trim, designated on the campus map as University Apartments, East and West. They fronted on Third Street, one of the main arteries of the older part of the campus, best known for its row of countless venerable sorority and fraternity houses. Bob had said he lived in the West apartments. I could just see the edge of the complex from where I stood.

My door suddenly flew open, startling me from my thoughts. "Surprise," I heard a voice say. I turned around and saw Mikki Barrett, my fifth-floor neighbor and new best friend, race into my room. Her shapely legs stretched up from the floor as she walked. Her almond-shaped eyes, full, rich mouth, and long, straight hair parted in the center gave her beauty an exotic edge, inspiring young men to twist their necks and stare in open appreciation.

"Welcome back," I said warmly, happy to discover she had cut her break short.

"Another storm," she blurted as she collapsed, winded, into my arms, "is on its way. Thought I should get back before I got snowed in!"

"Boy, am I glad you did," I said, giving her a hug.

We caught up a bit. She filled me in on her family and boyfriend in her hometown of Indianapolis. I told her briefly about the last week of being trapped in Bloomington. For Mikki and me, talk came easily, though today I only half listened to her, my thoughts full of a lanky stranger.

"Boyfriend . . . new job . . . vacation . . ." I caught only scattered words as Mikki spoke of her week. Then she stopped. "Jana, are you listening to me?"

"Yes. Of course I'm listening. It's only that I'm

on my way to take a guitar lesson. There's this
guy . . ." my voice trailed off.

The sparkle in my eyes sent Mikki into a
squeal of delight and demands for complete information. As I related the events of the past
evening and how I had met Bob, the words ea-
gerly pushed past my throat.

"He's offered to give me a guitar lesson at his
apartment," I announced, "and, believe it or not,
it's right over there." I pointed out the window
to West University Apartments. She gazed past
my finger.

"Jana." Mikki's voice was suddenly subdued.
"Those places are for *married* students!"

"Married students? No, they couldn't be. He's
not married." My mind refused to accept what
Mikki was saying.

She had to be mistaken. Robert Waller, who
sang of love in distant places with eyes that
beckoned me to come along, couldn't be *married*.
I'd watched the fingers of his left hand as they
moved up and down the ebony neck of his guitar and I was sure he wore no wedding ring. I
gave my friend a half smile. Mikki had to be
wrong.

"Just be careful, okay?" Mikki said, her voice

filled with concern. I felt her fingers digging into my arm as she held on, as if she were trying to protect me from my own instincts.

I nodded and promised to meet her for dinner, then hoisted my guitar case and set out for my first lesson, completely unaware that my life was about to change forever.

As I walked down the long corridor, into the elevator, across the lobby, and out the back door, Mikki's warning was still on my mind. A blast of cold afternoon air slapped at my face but couldn't numb my thoughts as I trudged through the snow that covered the grassy area known as Kinsey Hollow. *What if Mikki is right?* I thought. What if I'm on my way to see not one, but two Wallers? What am I getting myself into? I looked around and saw I had shuffled a wide, circular pattern in the snow. I stopped and leaned up against a tree to think. I knew I had already fallen for this man without even knowing him. And he had seemed interested in me. True, he hadn't actually said so, but it was in his eyes. Or at least I thought it was. Had I been wrong? Well, I decided, I wasn't going to find out standing frozen to a tree. I pushed myself forward and tromped out a straight path toward the West University Apartments.

My heart was pounding as I opened the glass door of the apartment building; I didn't know whether it was the result of exertion or anxiety. It didn't matter. I was determined to reach his apartment and put an end to the questions lodged, immobile, in my mind. The sound of my heels on the brown linoleum tile echoed throughout the dark hallways, shattering the silence. Noise in empty space, bouncing, reworking itself until it picked up its own rhythm.

Then I was there. Standing in front of his door, hand poised to knock, yet frozen in place. Curious. Frightened. If I hadn't heard the familiar strumming of guitar strings coming from the other side of the door, I might have lost my nerve. Instead, the sound held the same captivating pull it had the last time it passed my way, and once again, I was in its trap, unable, unwilling to turn away.

I gulped and knocked softly, tentatively. The music halted and I heard footsteps approaching the door. Again my heart raced, trying unsuccessfully to keep pace with my mind. And then he was before me, his blue eyes welcoming me inside.

"Hi," he said, his lips parting into that incredible smile. Moving aside to allow me to enter, he held the door with one hand, his guitar secure in the other. As my mouth opened into conversation, my eyes darted around the apartment. Canvassing, observing. No sign of a woman or a woman's touch. It appeared to be the home of a man without attachment. The look of bachelor living. A tiny kitchen to the right. A hint of dishes in the sink. To the left, a bedroom. Ahead, a short hallway and the living room.

There was a spartan quality about the place. It lacked the warmth of soft fabric and fresh flowers. Women's things. Gentle things. The hard edges of a wood-framed sofa were flanked by matching end tables with matching lamps. The single window in the room held a variety of small plants on the sill, budding in the small sliver of sunlight escaping from the edge of an exterior awning.

He motioned for me to come into the living room. A brick-and-plank bookshelf nearly four feet high extended out from the hallway and was piled high with volumes arranged neatly by size in precise order. Opposite the sofa was a stereo, bordered by hundreds of records. Next to it, a slab of wood bridged a pair of sawhorses and formed a desk, rough and perfect in its simplicity. Books and papers, scattered in a patchwork of organized chaos, covered the desktop, with a small desk lamp and a can of beer for company. I saw an ashtray and a pack of cigarettes. I couldn't detect the warm smell of last night's home-cooked dinner. Or a soft cologne. No scent of hair spray. No souvenir photographs of warm embraces. Nothing to suggest a woman lived here. So Mikki was wrong after all. My shoulders dropped in relief.

"How about a beer?" Bob asked, breaking into my internal dialogue. "Or a Coke?"

"Beer's great," I said. He went into the kitchen. I set my guitar down and removed my coat, suddenly self-conscious about what I was wearing. In my rush to get out of the dorm, I forgot to change. I was wearing the same tight jeans and suede boots I'd worn the night before. Only my black crewneck sweater was different, and it was an old one. I hoped he wouldn't notice.

A moment later he was back, a beer can in one hand, a chair in the other. I took the beer and he took my coat, draping it across the back of my chair, which he placed directly opposite his desk chair. As we settled into our respective seats, I noticed a number of basketball trophies lined properly across the back of the bookshelf. I pointed to them.

"What are these?" I asked.

"Laurels from another time," he smiled. "Another time, another place."

"Looks like you did pretty well."

"Yeah, I did, and it's funny because I never particularly liked the game," he said. "I'd spend hours shooting baskets—maybe two or three hundred a day. I did it for my dad." He shrugged. "He's a big basketball fan. That's why I played."

"He must be proud. Your father, I mean." My thoughts wandered as I reflected on things I'd done to please my mother. Unfortunately, I'd never seemed to get it right. She was such a perfectionist and I was such a gypsy.

He nodded. "I got a basketball scholarship to the University of Iowa. Quit after a year, though. Transferred over to University of Northern Iowa in Cedar Falls."

I started to ask what his father had to say about the shift of colleges and the dropping of the sport, but thought better of it. Personal experience had taught me well how the goals of parents and children often differ.

"How about you?" he asked. "Where are you from?"

"Here in Indiana. Up near Lake Michigan."

"You ever been to Iowa?" he asked.

I nodded, though I didn't bother to mention that my view of his home state was no more than a glimpse from the backseat of my father's car as it sped west on Route 80 toward Denver.

"It's great country. Rolling green fields. Long, dusty roads and winding rivers. Pure and uncomplicated." He turned to face me, expecting a reply. Having none, I quickly took a sip of my beer and smiled. His pale blue eyes crinkled at the corners as he remembered his Iowa, and he returned my smile.

"I'm afraid I'm a city girl," I ventured, selecting my words carefully, not wanting to challenge him. "Chicago, to be exact. The city lights, the elevated trains. There's an excitement in meeting strangers," I said, gathering courage from the thought of it. "And there's a rhythm to the city."

He nodded, but I knew he really didn't share my views. There was something about this man that told me he was definitely a country boy, a frontiersman, an explorer of the unknown and untarnished. He was too polite to tell me what he really thought of the big city, with its dirt and complications. I imagined that honking horns were an intrusion in his world of fields and pastures, but that he accepted and tolerated them for what they gave to others.

"Lake Michigan is there," I added, attempting to reveal my love for nature as well. "I've spent hours sunning on the sand dunes, watching the waves. There's a peaceful feeling there."

Though I couldn't see them, the differences between us were fundamental and dramatic. But as I sat on a wooden chair in his apartment with its bachelor furnishings, his knees only inches from mine, I could only stretch to find our similarities, our mutual love of music and the fact that I had younger twin brothers who played basketball.

"So let's see this guitar of yours," he said, taking another sip from his beer before setting it aside.

I got up, fetched my old guitar case, and handed it to him. Gently opening the case, Bob lifted the instrument into his lap, smiling in appreciation at what he discovered. In contrast to the battered case, my guitar was a well-preserved Martin, not unlike his own. An old Martin D-18. Full-bodied and rich.

As I watched him play it, bringing it to life, I related the story of how such a fine, old instrument came into my possession.

"I started playing guitar in the seventh grade," I said as he tuned the strings. "I had this inexpensive guitar. The tone was shallow and the strings were set so high that my fingers nearly bled trying to force them to the neck."

"We've all had one of those at one time or another," he laughed, cranking the fourth string tighter to correct the pitch. "Go on," he said, moving on to the fifth string.

"Well, I had this friend named Mary. She would come by in the afternoon and listen to me play," I continued as he listened to the tone of the string. It was still a little flat. "One day, while we were out shopping for songbooks, we spotted this wonderful old Martin. The store owner said that it had belonged to a left-handed country singer named Hank. See," I said, pointing to the top of the guitar. "He glued his name on the body there. There's still a shadow where the letters were."

Bob shook his head in disapproval as he studied the blond finish, rubbing his hand gently over the surface. Like me, he couldn't imagine anyone defacing an instrument. He turned his attention to the sixth and final string. It tuned easily and he began to accompany my story with a soft melody. The notes were deep and smooth and filled the room.

"Anyway, to my astonishment, Mary got her father to buy the guitar for her. I wanted to be jealous, but she was too good a friend. Besides, she offered to let me play it anytime I wanted."

"So how did you get it?" he asked, continuing to play.

"It wasn't long before Mary lost interest, and the guitar found itself buried under her bed with dust balls for company. I offered to buy it with my baby-sitting money." That brought a smile to his lips.

"Looks like you've babied her."

"It's a *him*," I teased. "His name is Yuri."

"Yuri?" Bob asked, looking up.

"I named him after the main character in my favorite film."

"Oh, yes, *Doctor Zhivago?*"

I nodded. Little did I realize then how much my life would soon closely parallel that classic love story, which had had such a powerful impact on me.

"I've oiled his neck religiously, and I keep trying to polish away the name Hank," I explained.

He smiled with appreciation for my efforts before turning his attention back to the guitar, picking the strings skillfully. My awe translated into a renewed resolve to master the instrument, as his fingers dazzled me with their swift and intricate pattern. Finally relinquishing Yuri back into my care, he picked up his own guitar and began our lesson.

Deliberate and gentle in manner, he taught as he spoke, clearly and simply, without wasted words. I learned the basics of the Travis picking pattern that day, trying to concentrate on his instructions rather than the tiny blond hairs on his forearm that caught the afternoon sunlight as it beamed into the living room window and across the assortment of potted plants. His fingers flew over and over through the Travis pattern, moving like quicksilver through a series of intricate steps.

Later, when the beer was gone and the sunlight had begun to fade, we looked at each other and knew it was time to wrap things up, though neither of us was anxious for the afternoon to end. He told me he thought I'd done just fine and sent me home with the advice to try practicing in the dark to concentrate on the rhythm of the music rather than the position of my fingers. I wanted to reach out and touch him, but instead I merely thanked him for the lesson as he walked me to the door.

"Why don't you come back next Saturday and we'll see how you do?"

I didn't have to think twice. "I'll be here at two o'clock."

"Great," he said. "See you then."

I nodded and smiled a smile that lasted all the way across Kinsey Hollow, glancing back at his building several times, knowing he was inside, still playing his songs of sadness and love.

* * *

"So-o-o?" Mikki asked that night, wanting to hear every detail as we sat in Curry House, the name given to our wing of the dormitory.

"He's not married," I said, getting to the bottom line and putting an end to her frustration.

"But West University Apartments—"

"I know," I stopped her in midsentence, "are for married students. Well, there was no wife, or even a picture of a girlfriend. There wasn't a lacy curtain or tablecloth or stray bobby-pin. If he was married, he's gotten a divorce. The university must still let him live there." It was the only explanation I could think of that made sense, and even Mikki had to agree that it sounded logical.

I ate only half my dinner, unable to keep my concentration on food when there was a new picking pattern to learn and a new friend to impress. I kept company with Yuri for the rest of the evening, practicing in the dark just as instructed, before finally falling asleep with the guitar in my arms.

The days moved on, one after another, as I plodded through classes, saving my enthusiasm for my next lesson with Bob. I practiced nightly and by the time Saturday arrived I was good enough on the Travis pattern to join my teacher, mentor, and lover of dusty roads in duets. The sound of our guitars melded with a passion, and his voice sang folk songs that harped of sagas of the heart.

His taste in music centered on pure folk rather than the popular protest songs that I knew and had played in high school in front of audiences in the thousands. Songs of peace were surefire audience pleasers and I performed them easily, even if I didn't stop to fully comprehend their meaning. Bob, however, had no time for songs of war, forbidden violence, or white doves flapping wings of hope. His was a world of forgotten ponds and covered bridges, where men touched out of kindness, not hostility, and women revealed desires long suppressed.

Although the campus was erupting with the antiwar activities of the Students for a Democratic Society, I was only beginning to understand the horrors of the Vietnam War. That is how, in February of 1967, I could sit content and at peace in the West University Apartments, learning about the origins of folk music from someone who had devoted himself to the subject.

Each Saturday lesson would reveal new bits and pieces of this man who stood alone in my heart. For all the romance in his songs, his life was one of numbers and formulas. Academically he was pursuing a doctorate in business management. His mind worked well with theories, he said, and he had hopes of becoming a teacher at a university in Iowa. He talked of molding minds and changing the system for the better. His bookshelves, which should have held first editions, classic reprints, and the complete poetry of W. B. Yeats, were instead lined with textbooks on mathematics, economics, logistics, and business management. There was little to remind him of the loveliness of Iowa among the equations of projected displacement. But somehow I knew he remembered.

There was never any talk of friends on campus, though he often mentioned his friend Scott from back home. But in Bloomington, Indiana, it seemed as if his entire world existed within the walls of West University Apartments. No phone calls to interrupt our sessions, no surprise visitors knocking on the door. Our hours together were private lessons in life, explored through music.

His enormous record collection became the highway on which we would travel across time and lands, listening to albums selected with great care and dissecting the meaning of song lyrics. To these he added his own melodies, written with the same precision as his mathematical formulas. No room for a stray word or an improper note.

I will always remember one particular Saturday. I learned he had been struggling for several weeks with a song he'd been writing, attempting to find the correct name for its heroine.

"Mind if I try using Jana?" he asked.

"No, I don't think so," I said. Then I caught the double entendre and laughed. "Should I?"

He laughed, too, as he realized what he'd said. At that moment I felt so smitten with this man, I would have given him my name and chosen another if I'd thought he would find it to his liking. Take my name, explore it, use it. And, in response to the double meaning, don't stop there. The rest of me is available as well. I blushed as the thought worked its way through my mind. He must have seen it, because his laughter faded into a soft smile and his eyes grew momentarily intense.

"Well, let's hear it," I said, breaking the mood deliberately to hide my sudden nervousness, wondering if the moment was as special to him as it was to me.

"Okay. If you say so." Bob studied the music and added a few words with a pen, then began singing.

When Jana was young, restless was she
Like a willow she caressed the wind.
And as crystal autumn mornings fade into dusty
afternoons,
She passed my way and was gone again.

He sang the ballad looking into my eyes, and at that moment I wanted to throw my arms around him and confess my love, pledge my devotion, swear to him that this Jana would never disappear on the breath of an autumn wind.

"I like it. It works," he said, after finishing the next few verses of the song. Smiling a self-effacing grin, he added, "Thanks."

That night I replayed the moment in my heart, thinking about the path our relationship had taken. In the weeks since we'd met, there had been no walks in the moonlight, no romantic candlelight dinners, no warm, passionate kisses, no holding hands in the doorway. Instead, I had fallen deeply in love by sitting on the floor with him, playing the guitar or listening to folk music, and was abundantly happy when we shared a salami sandwich, a can of beer, and some hot potato soup he prepared fresh from a can. And now a song, "When Jana Was Young." I was sure I was the luckiest girl in the world.

A few more gentle Saturdays passed and with them came the knowledge that we both shared an affection for the music of Ian and Sylvia, the Canadian duo who sang the song "Red Velvet." They used vocal harmony in a distinctive way, one Bob thought the two of us could duplicate.

Moving on the notion, we arranged to meet especially early the following Saturday. The days moved in sporadic lunges, the clock ticking down the hours until the appointed time. There must have been pavement beneath my feet as I walked to the apartment that Saturday, but I was so thrilled by the thought of singing with him that I felt I was moving on air.

The first breeze of spring caressed my face and inched inside my jacket through sleeves and hem. It chilled my body but not my excitement as I raced across Kinsey Hollow and up the sidewalk, just as I had done so many times before. As usual, Bob was waiting, practicing, singing.

Down the short hallway, past the kitchen and bedroom, into the living room. We plunged into practice so quickly and naturally that I didn't think to notice that something was out of place. It wasn't until we had been singing a respectable imitation of Ian and Sylvia for over half an hour when the bedroom door opened. Only then did I realize that for the first time, the door had been closed and we were not alone.

I turned my head with his in the direction of the sound and saw an incredibly beautiful woman standing in the hallway. Dark eyes shined through flawless skin. She wore no makeup and needed none. Her brilliant smile cut a swath across her face, edged by long, dark, silky hair that nearly reached down to her hips. She broke into applause as she stepped forward.

"Bravo," she raved in critical appreciation.

Standing now, Robert Waller of the gentle eyes and beautiful songs, the molder of minds and spinner of dreams, uttered words that seared my heart with the fire of a stoked brand-ing iron and left a mark I thought would never heal.

"Jana, this is my wife, Georgia." Turning toward her, he continued, "Georgia, meet Jana."

I was short of breath, my lungs refusing to expand. The room felt suddenly close and warm. He talked, she talked. An exchange of smiles, a kiss on the cheek. He helped her on with her coat; she mentioned working late at the bookstore. She waved a little good-bye; my fingers waved back. And without the slightest care, she left the apartment. In less than a min-ute, my world had ended.

He was sitting again, beginning to play. My mind was blank as I sank to the floor, autopilot assuming control, following his lead wherever it took me.

Jana. Those places are for married students. Married students. Married students. Mikki's words raced through my mind.

Stupid. Stupid. Stupid. I repeated the word silently to myself, hearing my blood pounding through a system on overload. The love of my life was now a fantasy in which I was the only character. Robert Waller, graduate student and folk singer, had only been trying to help a budding guitarist. The rest was a silly teenager's imagination, the stuff of romance novels and poetry.

When I got ready to leave that day, I was walked to the door in the usual way, down the short hallway, past the bedroom and kitchen. At the door, instead of reaching for the knob, I saw his hand move toward my face and felt it warm against my neck. He rubbed it gently, purposely lingering beyond polite innocence.

I turned to face him as our eyes met and embraced. Mine silently questioned; his gave an answer. But I was now too unsure of my instincts to try to interpret it.

FOUR

Gentle Afternoons

But until that day when it comes
April will hum a little tune
And deep down inside where the special feelings
    must hide
We'll remember our gentle afternoons.

As I made my way back to the dorm that afternoon, the steady pace of my footsteps clashed with the uneven rhythm of my thoughts. I was unaware of the path I walked or the people I passed. I kept seeing Georgia standing in the doorway, her long, dark hair shining, her innocent smile suspecting nothing. And why should she suspect anything? Nothing had happened, except in the halls of a teenager's active imagination. And nothing was going to happen.

Entering Read Center, I stepped into the elevator and watched the doors shut. I could not block the image of Georgia or her elegant beauty from my mind. Sometime during my preteen years, I had become aware that the world was full of people prettier than I was. I had no appreciation of my northern European heritage. Summers spent at the beach attempting to tan my pale skin had left me freckled. I was cute. I was thin. But I never thought of myself as pretty, let alone Georgia Waller beautiful.

Years of swimming had given me long muscles that made my legs appear longer, and I'd shortened the hems on all my skirts as soon as I'd arrived at school. With blond highlights added to my hair by one of the girls on the third floor, I'd succeeded in altering my appearance to the point that I was beginning to attract attention.

But these external changes, however nice, were merely quick fixes for a young woman who was unsure of who she was and if she had value. That is, until I had met Bob, who seemed to change everything quickly. More than a whimsical spinner of love songs, he had a keen perception and tender passion for the human condition. I felt so at ease with him in my life that for the first time ever, I dared to believe in my dreams. It was a new experience, this feeling, this love. Bob allowed me to be myself; he had accepted me for who I was. Or had he? *Of course he accepted you,* a voice in my head answered. *He accepted you as a skinny little kid who wanted to learn to play the guitar.*

As the elevator doors opened, I heard myself say, "Stupid! Stupid! Stupid!"

"What's stupid?" a voice came out of nowhere. Mikki was coming down the hall as I stepped out of the elevator. "What's stupid?" she repeated.

The sight of my friend flooded my eyes and my heart with tears. The warning she had given me before my first trip to visit Bob beat mercilessly at my mind. Seeing my condition, she took me by the arm and accompanied me to my room in silence.

"Want to talk about it?" she asked as I closed the door behind us. Mikki had a wonderful capacity to question without prying, to support without suppressing.

"You were right," I said. "I met his wife today."

The words leaving my mouth began a flood of truth. Mikki sat opposite me on my roommate Judy's bed, listening silently, patiently, as I paced the floor, relating the events of the past several hours. She was a neutral sounding board, neither commenting nor criticizing, until I reached the point where I left Bob's apartment, suddenly overcome with self-doubt.

"Now wait just a minute," she said, interrupting. Her long legs uncurled from beneath her and she stood to look me in the eye. "The problem isn't you. The problem is that the guy is married. That's not your fault."

She did her best to reinforce my self-image, reminding me of my relationship with a handsome Italian freshman named Marc Bertelli, which had blossomed and thrived until I had followed my heart to West University Apartments.

I thought briefly about Marc and how he had swaggered into my life dressed in a white T-shirt that hugged a muscled chest, faded jeans, and combat boots. His long, wavy black hair, brown-black eyes, and olive skin were complimented by a brilliant smile that flashed like a signal flare when we first met.

"You're beautiful," he whispered to me on our first date. Perfect words to bolster any young woman. After dating him steadily for six weeks, I found myself lying beside him on a blanket under the trees in the silvery moonlight.

"You're beautiful," he said again, his voice catching slightly in his throat.

I remembered how the words had played in my mind like a symphony, and I clung to them as I did to him. He stroked my hair and continued to whisper in and kiss at my ear, pushing his hand up under my sweater and over my breast. I was a virgin but ready to explore my sexuality, and he was more than happy to guide me through uncharted terrain. Though I had cared for Marc, what I felt for Bob was different, deeper.

"What's happening with him, anyway?" Mikki asked.

"We're still friends," I said with a shrug. "Actually, he called last week. He's pledging Tau Kappa Epsilon and they're having a party this Friday."

Mikki smiled in excitement. "This could be good. Why don't you concentrate on a relationship you're sure of, instead of one that can only mean trouble?"

I turned the idea around in my head, eventually admitting to her, and more importantly to myself, that I had no relationship with Bob. He was the teacher, I was the pupil, and our only source of attraction was our mutual love for guitar. That was it. It had to be. I had been acting foolish and my imagination had run away with me.

"I hope it's your imagination. 'Cause if it isn't, you could be in for some pretty heavy stuff," Mikki added ominously.

I went to the sink, turned on the tap, and splashed my face with cold water. Deep breaths came next and, finally, some sense of relaxation settled in as I patted my skin dry, closing my eyes against the warmth of the towel. It was going to take me a while to completely process Mikki's last words. I had been so worried that Bob didn't like me that I had never considered what would happen if he really did.

Later that night at dinner, the subject entered and reentered my mind, refusing to be dismissed. Despite the conversation around me, my thoughts were of Bob, of his passion for dusty roads and winding rivers that carved into new frontiers and unexpected adventure, of the sound of his voice as he sang of gentle nights and sweet rain. Moving, always moving, in search of something unknown.

The days that followed piled one on top of the other as my head and heart engaged in a tug-of-war between the rational and emotional. My heart could no more give up Bob than it could stop beating, yet my brain kept insisting that giving him up was the only thing to do. By Friday night I had come to the uneasy realization that we would not be seeing one another again.

There would be one last phone call, of course, with fervent excuses and abundant thanks. That would happen tomorrow. At the moment, however, I concentrated on my makeup and attempted to generate enthusiasm for my date with Marc at the Tau Kappa Epsilon house. My enthusiasm was contrived and sat heavy in my stomach. Still, I had given Marc my word, and Mikki as well. Lipstick, mascara, a touch of perfume, and I was beginning to feel better about the situation when the telephone rang.

"Jannie?" the voice questioned.

It was my mother. The sound of her voice was sharp and directed. Customary.

"Mother?" I answered, making no attempt to hide my surprise.

"I'm at the Student Union hotel and I want you to come over here right away."

It wasn't a request. It was a command. Something was wrong. My mother had made the six-hour trip from Munster to deliver some news, and that could only mean it was bad. Good news is easy to say over the phone. Bad news is the stuff of personal appearances and "sit down" prefaces. My plans would have to be put on hold. I told her I'd be there in fifteen minutes. Time enough to fret about aged relatives, family strife, past improprieties, white lies, and anything else I could conjure up to explain her unannounced arrival. Time enough to call Marc and tell him not to expect me to arrive at the appointed hour. He was disappointed but understanding in an uncharacteristically adult way. "Come when you can," he said without argument. "And good luck with your mom."

"Okay, thanks," I replied.

I took the shortcut to the Union, the same path I had taken with Jane and the others months before when we headed to the Kiva that cold night in January. By the time I reached the heavy glass doors of the hotel entrance, I was out of breath and short on nerves. When I arrived at her room, I was in even worse shape.

She answered the knock on the door without a smile or even a greeting, causing my heart to miss one beat, then two. Was it still beating at all? Her look told me it wasn't the death of a grandparent or a problem with my brothers that had brought her to Bloomington. The problem was me, and she made it very clear that I was in trouble. Big trouble.

She turned her back to me, forcing me to follow her, then motioned toward a chair as she sat on the bed.

"Mother?" I questioned. "What is it?"

Her face was rigid as she opened her purse and took out a letter. She held it out in my direction.

"This came in the mail for you. I thought it might be important so I opened it, planning to read it to you over the phone. But I think you had better read it yourself."

Heart beating fast now. Faster. Faster still,

without consideration for flow or pressure. I slowly took the envelope and turned it over, reading the return address. It was from Danny Mosley, a boy I'd dated in high school. This is what brought my mother to Bloomington? This was what was important enough to open and read? I felt violated and angry but apprehensive. I struggled not to let it show.

When I had first met Danny I was a sophomore and he was a senior. He was all hands and hormones in the front seat of his parked convertible and I spent several hours rejecting his advances before he finally gave up and called it quits. I was never to hear from him again.

Or at least not until last Christmas, when our paths crossed by a mere accident of timing and ironic fate. In the three years that had passed, his hormones had tempered little, if any, and my new look impressed him. He took advantage of the chance meeting and asked me for a date.

Rather than admit I would rather spend every Saturday night alone for life than date him again, I declined his offer politely with a casual excuse that centered on my new boyfriend at college. I made the relationship with Marc sound more serious than it was, and though he didn't much like the rejection, he had little choice but to accept it. Or so I thought.

Fabrications, even for the best of reasons, have a way of breeding their own contempt. In this case, my exaggerated relationship with Marc became an instant liability, festering in Danny's mind until he produced venom in the form of the letter I now held.

It shook slightly in my hand, which was trembling in spite of my best efforts to keep it steady. As I began to read its contents, I could feel the hard, cold stare of my mother's eyes pierce through me. Danny wrote with rage uncontrolled, speaking of my college friend and the virginity I had no doubt given up to him.

His words reeked of hurt ego and lost pride as he suggested I would have been better off giving in to him years earlier, since he was so experienced and I was so naive. Now, he figured, I would probably make the mistake of getting pregnant. Under other circumstances, I would have laughed at his pompous vulgarity.

But under the harsh glare of my mother's eyes, I succumbed to the humiliation she wanted me to feel. Our distant relationship had not improved with my teenage years. The older

I got, the more I realized completely and un-equivocally how totally disappointed she was in her only daughter. Although it would always hurt deeply, I slowly began to understand the underlying reasons for her lack of affection toward me. Our dreams for others can never really come true, and I had often driven that point home in broad strokes across the dry can-vas of my mother's hopes. And I was about to do it again.

It took little time and effort to convince her the letter was merely the jealous raving of a spurned teenager. Such was not the case, how-ever, when it came to explaining away my rela-tionship with Marc. My mother had met him at an Indiana football game in the fall, and her cold, unbending tone suggested that she had sensed sexual undercurrents.

At first, I tried to talk around the subject. It wasn't an easy one for me to discuss with her, even in the best of times. I attempted to dodge and play through the moment, giving informa-tion without saying too much. She wasn't buy-ing my act of naiveté, though, and it showed. She stared pointedly, unmoving, in that special way mothers have with daughters that says they've been there before and know all the tricks.

Trapped by my fear of her, I wanted to run, to escape the hot lights in the small room that I was certain were revealing the truth written across my face. Instead, I gathered the small remnants of my rapidly deteriorating courage and told her the truth. Reaching out not just to my mother, but to another woman, I aimed at opening a channel of understanding, hoping that honesty would bridge the chasm that had separated us almost from birth.

"Marc and I have had sex—a few times. When I thought I really cared for him. I've been taking birth control pills, so you don't need to worry. I honestly believed I was in love with him. And that he loved me."

The net of hope I threw my mother's way was not caught that night. She didn't even reach out for it. She riled in anger and hurt, lamenting her failure as a parent, wondering where she had gone wrong in raising me as a proper young lady. My honesty was rewarded with criticism, the kind that starts low and slowly builds into anguish as all the pieces topple into a heap.

Instead of bonding with a woman I had

longed to know, I'd driven the wedge between us even deeper, hurting us both in the process. I had done nothing wrong, yet I felt awful. A victim of a generation gap that approached this subject on different levels, from different worlds.

Talked out and emotionally empty, I was coldly dismissed. I left and walked to the TKE house, where loud music, harsh laughter, and the smell of alcohol greeted me. *God, I hate this,* I thought as I walked through the crowd. I ached at having to go through the motions of being there, ached for an understanding shoulder to cry on. Instead, I found Marc—gorgeous, toned, and smiling—eager to have me join in the party.

No mention of my being upset. No words of consolation or solace. A mixture of grain alcohol and soda pop was shoved in my hand. It would help me loosen up, Marc said. Change my mood, he said. Make me feel better. The sweetness slipped into my system, first satisfying, then numbing a mind already on overload. One drink, then another. It all seemed pretty harmless. As minutes grew into hours and the party mellowed into sensuous pockets of romance, I tried to tell Marc what had happened with my mother.

Poor, perfect, plastered Marc. Like his fraternity brothers, his chief concern was to engage in the rites of pledgehood: bedding a maiden and calling her his own. He knew nothing of my feelings for Bob, only that I had become increasingly distant since the first of the year. The alcohol had charged his libido and he blindly hoped it had had the same effect on me. When I needed comfort and hugs of compassion, he offered only sex. It was both revealing and disgusting. Pushing, running, I left the TKE house behind me that night, and Marc with it.

Unable to focus, head pulsing with the rush of liquor and emotion, I walked along unlit sidewalks, willing myself by sheer force of determination to return to the safety and solace of my dorm room. There I lapsed into a dead sleep, grateful for the lack of thoughts or dreams.

The following morning the sun's strong rays woke me early and challenged me to rise. My head was pounding with the force of machinery, industrial gauge, heavy weight. It was nothing compared to the sickness I felt toward myself, not to mention toward the men in my life.

I thought about Bob. It was Saturday. He would be expecting me. I needed to make my call to him. I wouldn't have to lie. I was sick; I was tired. If nothing else, life had provided me with the perfect excuse to skip my guitar lesson. When I explained I wasn't feeling well, Bob's concern sounded genuine. He asked what was wrong, how he could help.

"I just need to rest," was the best I could do.

When he pressed further, our conversation turned to fraternity parties and strange drinks and unsuspecting young women who had no business being there to begin with. He listened without commenting until I finished.

"Not very smart," he said, without a trace of condemnation in his tone. He said he understood, politely indicated he hoped I'd feel better soon, and hung up the phone. I don't know what I was expecting, but I was convinced that I had just scratched another man off my fast shrinking list of friends.

I should have felt relief wash over me, despite

my hangover. I had just been dropped by the man I had planned never to see again. Yet satisfaction eluded me. In its place was an emptiness I knew I would be hard-pressed to fill.

The telephone rang and I whirled in response as floor, walls, and ceiling swirled around me and I collapsed in the middle of the rug. The sound was intense, amplified tenfold by the sensitive receptors in my brain, placed on alert by the unrelenting pressure of the hangover from hell.

I reached for the phone. "Hullo," I said weakly from my position on the floor.

"I've given this situation a second thought." It was Bob's voice, gentle and kind. "Come on over here. Just this once," he said with a hint of humor, "I've decided to help you."

I moaned that I couldn't move. He replied that I could if I put my mind to it. He had a variety of miracle cures guaranteed to make me feel better.

My mind was aching itself into a response, searching for an excuse that wasn't there, not wanting to find it. My weak legs and queasy stomach were another story.

"I don't think I can walk that far," I said honestly, feeling nausea creeping into place and preparing for a rapid assault.

His laugh was warm and soothed my heart with its understanding.

"Crawl if you have to," was his only reply. "And you can leave your guitar at home today. I doubt you're going to want to play."

Too miserable to think, I whispered, "I'll be there," and hung up the phone. I made an attempt to brush my teeth, though my stomach was not in favor of the idea. I don't remember what clothes I put on, but I knew I'd look awful no matter what I wore, so I didn't care. Besides, there was no point in trying to impress him anymore, even if I felt good.

I walked slowly down the hall, into the elevator, and out the lobby door, careful to keep my equilibrium as I went. The brisk spring air buoyed me upright, but I directed my eyes away from the sun and toward the ground ahead. Momentum alone kept me moving as I navigated Kinsey Hollow and pushed forward, up the stairs and down the hall, to Bob's apartment.

As I knocked on his door, I heard soft music

playing, and then suddenly he was there. Smiling, greeting, welcoming me into his home gently. There were no recriminations, no lectures on drinking, not even any further questions about the previous night. He guided me quietly into the bedroom, where I sank onto the soft rug on the floor.

The room was flooded by amber light, which poured delicately through the closed curtains, accented by the soft glow of a desk lamp. He left me there, only to reappear a moment later with an aspirin and a beer. The sight of more booze made my stomach roll, with my eyes following.

I made no attempt to argue, following his instructions to down the aspirin with the cold, frothy beverage. The flavor hung on my throat, my mouth, my lips. But it did not make me sick as I had feared. Instead, I felt soothed and calm in the moments that followed, helped along by the gentleness in his eyes.

Then he was gone once more. The sound of rattling utensils suggested he was back in the kitchen, preparing one of his secret miracle cures that would soon rescue me from my self-indulged purgatory of excess. As I sat and smiled inwardly at his kindness, my eyes roamed the room. His room. Her room.

The bedroom door formed one side of a corner, the other side being the door to the bathroom. I was facing a chest of drawers that stood against a short wall between the bathroom and a closet. Beside me, on a long wall, was a table upon which rested the small desk lamp, a photo, a pad, and a pen. Next to it was a stool.

Behind me, a neatly made double bed. His bed. Her bed. It caught my eyes and held them until I lowered them once more, ashamed of myself for allowing my mind to imagine what it would be like to make love to him. A single draped window was centered on the wall alongside the bed, and a cushioned chair and second chest of drawers completed the decor. The area rug I was sitting on covered the dark floor and added to the room's soft mood.

"A miracle cure." Bob's voice interrupted my silence as he returned to the room with some warm soup. I pushed a small smile into place and took the soup bowl from his extended hand as he folded himself down next to me, his long legs grazing mine in the process.

The soup was indeed a magic potion. "Feeling better?" he asked after a time.

"Much," I responded, and thanked him.

He got up and sat in the cushioned chair, motioning for me to move over and sit in front of him. Gently he rubbed my shoulders, working his fingers up my neck to the base of my skull. Then he tilted my head back into his lap and began massaging my temples. It was so soothing that I closed my eyes and felt the last traces of my headache melt away. My mouth relaxed into a smile of contentment. I barely noticed when he shifted his position and moved my head just a bit. I lifted my eyelids only slightly in response, but it was enough to see his face very near, just before I felt his lips on mine.

His kiss was soft and gentle. He moved slowly at first, then more passionately as his strong hands cradled my face, pulling me closer. He released his hold and moved off the chair, pausing to look deep into my eyes with such intense longing, it made me shiver. Seeing this, he pulled back, teasing me a moment before moving his body close to mine and kissing me again, his lips full and tender. *It wasn't my imagination after all,* I thought before surrendering to him completely. I was lost and I was found, and I would never be the same again. Our love had come from nowhere and had nowhere to go, except some special dimension belonging only to us.

Lips parted now, we shared the thoughts and feelings of love, building on the moment our eyes first met.

"I hadn't wanted to look at you, you know," I confessed, thinking of that night at the Kiva. "I was afraid of what I was feeling."

"I know," he answered. "I felt it, too."

And with that, the conversation rolled and ebbed in a natural rhythm like foam carried on the top of the ocean tide, always moving but never disappearing. We spoke of parents and re-sponsibility. I told him I thought he had done a better job of fulfilling his parents' expectations than I had mine.

Tales from the past exposed with the advantage of hindsight poured from my mouth and into a room filled with complete understanding. There was no condemnation or disapproval, only sup-port and compassion. Feeling safe, I told him the details of my mother's unexpected visit.

"If you're such a lousy daughter, why do your

mother's feelings matter so much to you?" he asked gently.

I hadn't an answer, anymore than I did when he had praised my maturity, sensitivity, and worldliness. I was awed by his kindness, which tugged at my heart, and the warmth of his smile charged up my emotions with a renewed energy that tugged at my conscience. His words had helped revive my spirits, helped me lift that dark cloud of self-doubt from my mind.

He was forbidden territory in more than one way. Not only was he married, but his intensity was so strong that it caused my mind to flood with confusion at the prospect of dealing with it. Yet he drew me back, like a moth to a flame, with exactly the same kind of instinctive attraction.

We spoke of our music and chosen careers. I wondered aloud of his quest for a degree in business management at the expense of his love for gentler things. He thought it wiser that I concentrate on English rather than on my proclaimed major of elementary education.

Through it all, the one forgotten element was Georgia. His wife was missing physically and emotionally. He never brought up her name, and neither did I. Hours later, as I moved to leave, he pulled me close once again. We touched—no more than that—but it was soft and wonderful and built on a foundation so natural as to be unseen.

The person who walked away from his apartment that day was not the same person who entered. Robert had done more than fill my head with songs of love and dusty roads. He had given me back a piece of myself—my feeling of worth—I thought I had lost forever. With confidence renewed, I used the next few days to act on Bob's advice and work on changing my major, discovering it was an easy process that could be handled in the fall, with credit for my current classes fully transferrable.

The following Saturday, as I walked to the West University Apartments, the sweet scent of budding spring grass permeated the air around Kinsey Hollow. The last of the snow had melted away, and a freshness enveloped the university, buoying my new attitude about myself and my relationship with Bob. He was waiting, as usual, alone and with a cool beer in hand, smiling wide and broad and full of love.

After tuning our guitars, we headed into the

bedroom and sat on the floor to play. The setting gave us more room to maneuver, without the confines of the living room chairs. It also allowed for greater intimacy. Now, when our knees touched, it was deliberate. Each chord, each love song took on a special meaning—the notes, the words, the looks, bonding us for time eternal.

The shift from floor to bed was as instinctive as it was unplanned. The sunlight's amber glow near the bed was warm and inviting. We moved as one, helping each other shed our clothes. We lay naked on the bed, flesh against flesh. The boundaries between personal space had dissolved. No words, only thoughts, as our special telepathy flared into being, silently communicating what we were feeling in our hearts. We kissed long and deep, his warm hands on the small of my back. Our tongues darted sensuously in a dance of love. He took over now, dominating in a gentle way but with a passion so intense that no degree of experience or practiced technique would ever rival what we felt in each other's arms that day.

Clutching, moving, loving, our love unfolded in a perfectly synchronized ballet of emotion and impulse. Flashes of white skin that could tolerate no sun, hair damp with perspiration. Robert Waller, weaver of dreams and singer of love, uttered soft sounds of affection, and I returned them in kind.

With eyes closed now, we were transported to a magical place where lovers meet and desire rules. In that place, there was no sense of time or limitations imposed by a practical world. We were free to love, and when we returned from our time together, our lives moved forward with predictability: classes attended, coursework completed, and songs sung. Yet each time we returned to that special place, it welcomed us back as the long-lost lovers we were destined to become.

FIVE

April Rains

And the April rains, they are lonely rains
They fall from my eyes and onto the ground.
And the April rains are the only rains
That fall the whole year around.

This euphoria I was feeling, this unbridled exuberance for life, was beyond anything I had ever experienced. Pure. Unblemished. And short-lived.

One Saturday morning in late March, I walked to my lesson as I had for the past couple of weeks, my head full of Robert Waller, picking techniques, folk songs, and love. This was not going to be a typical Saturday, however, as I learned when Bob answered my knock on his door. In place of his bright smile was a solemn stare, and the usual kiss had been supplanted by a grim flick of his head, motioning me to come inside.

"Hi," I said in an unsure voice, my heart pounding, ready to burst out of my chest. Something was wrong. What?

"Hi," he answered tersely, turning his back on me and walking away as I closed the door and paused in the entry hall. "Just leave everything in there," he said, sweeping his arm toward the living room before disappearing into the bedroom.

A million frightening scenarios raced through my head as I rushed to comply. Guitar down by the bookcase, jacket tossed toward the couch, I pushed my body toward the bedroom. Each step was slower than the one before, and when I caught sight of Bob from the doorway, I came to a complete stop.

He was sitting on the stool next to the table, hands folded in his lap, his somber face bathed in the amber glow of the little desk lamp, which cast its warmth in defiance of the melancholy around it. His head was bent to the side as though he were listening to some distant sound, his eyes far off in another place. He held out his arms to me.

"Come on in." His voice was suddenly soft and gentle, and I felt a wave of relief as I quickly crossed the room into his embrace. He put his arms around my waist and I wrapped mine around his neck. I rested my head on his and closed my eyes. I wanted to absorb his pain, let him know that whatever it was, it would be all right as long as we still had our love.

Relaxing with his touch, I lifted my head to look into his eyes, ready to face the problem, no matter what it might be. Arms still around each other, he seated me on his knee and struggled for words.

"You know I've come to care very much for you," he began hesitantly. I nodded but said nothing. "I've even been thinking about leaving my wife."

Given the love that we shared, his words should have filled my heart with joy. Instead, my breath caught sharply in my throat. Now it was my turn to look off into the distance. I was thinking of everything and nothing at the same time. There was more; I could sense it. I didn't know what was coming next and I wasn't sure I wanted to hear it. Of all the things he could have said, his next words were the furthest from my mind.

"We found out yesterday that we're going to have a baby."

Still saying nothing, I pulled back to look at him. His eyes were full of pain and unable to meet mine.

"We've talked about having a family and always planned on it, only . . . it's just that we were going to wait until after I finished graduate school."

He fidgeted in his seat and I took the cue to move to the floor in front of him. His voice trailed off as he considered fatherhood with mixed emotions. My eyes never left his face, even as the first sparkle of a tear spilled onto his cheek. My heart ached to see him cry.

"I love you," he said, "but I need to stay in my marriage now." He had his responsibilities and knew it. I expected nothing less of him. I simply nodded as my own tears began to fall. He moved to the floor beside me, looked at me, and took my hands in his.

"I met her when she was only sixteen, and I am the only man she's ever known." His eyes moved to our hands, locked in a tight embrace. "She needs me. She'd be lost if I ever left her. And I do love her. It's a different love than I have for you. She fits me like an old shoe, comfortable, dependable. You're like a new shoe, all shiny and bright. This is so difficult, but I can't let her down. For the long run, my choice has to be the comfort of the old shoe."

He didn't ask for my understanding. He knew he had it. We continued to sit there, on the floor, with no more need for words. Bob began to relax some, now that the news had been broken. There on the floor in the West University Apartments, I held the hands of my teacher, lover, friend. Uncertain of our future, but bound by our past. I felt the tears welling up, but I fought them back, wanting to be strong, for him, for us.

I knew he was excited about the baby and, to be perfectly honest, I was, too. There could be no other reaction. I loved him. His joy was my joy; his sorrow, my sorrow. Love does not know jealousy and anger. Those things are elements of possession and control. Love is about fully accepting what is best for another. Sometimes it means holding on, sometimes it means letting go. From the moment I had met Georgia and knew that Robert Waller was married, it was clear that our time together would be brief. Intense, magical, but fleeting.

I moved my head against his chest and he held my hand. I traced his long fingers with mine, studying, memorizing every curve, every line. He would be gone soon. I realized that fully and completely and resolved to make the best use of every second remaining to us.

When we finally picked up our guitars that day, we played with a special compassion and empathy. When we sang of lost loves, the words were no longer impersonal lyrics about unknown emotions. Though we wouldn't make love that day, we shared our music as we would our passion and that was enough. As the afternoon wore on, we addressed our situation once more.

"I want us to keep going for as long as we can," he said. The weakening sun sent soft rays across the floor of the bedroom. "The baby isn't due until fall. But we can't continue unless we both know and accept that it must come to an end."

I nodded and hugged him. I agreed with him

completely but at that point couldn't fully com-prehend what it would come to mean. It was something that had to be lived to be under-stood. For today, though, it all seemed quite simple and reasonable and I was happy that we still would have some time together.

After I returned to the dorm, Mikki stopped by on her way to dinner. She sensed a passage, some deep change in me. I said nothing, feeling too close to the moment to discuss it with any-one. Later, lying in bed in my darkened room on the fifth floor of Curry House, I looked up at the drapes as though I could see out the window and across Kinsey Hollow to the West Univer-sity Apartments. His apartment. Her apartment.

A week later, as we took our places on the floor in the bedroom once more, Bob sang a new song, one he had written for me. It was entitled "April Rains." As I heard him sing, our tears flowed, uncontrolled, no longer censored for the sake of appearance.

Gone are the days when you and I would lay together,
Oh how the times did roll!
But soon, much too soon, the summertime had come
And bound separate ways were we . . .

He sang of how we would remember our quiet times together long after they were over. He sang of the April rains that would always remind us of each other. We returned to making love that day, slow and deeply passionate love with an added urgency, as if our physical bodies now knew what our minds had understood a week before. Eyes and hands moved together, memorizing each detail, storing the knowledge in the back roads of our minds for the lonely journey ahead.

In the coming weeks, we would move and blend in defiance of our self-imposed emotional deadline. We were spared the constant pressure it might otherwise have created by an invitation from the Acacia fraternity to perform at their annual ice cream social at the end of May. The brothers of Acacia had asked Bob to sing and he extended the invitation to include me.

There would be weeks of rehearsal after selecting songs and deciding on arrangements. Finally, in late April, Bob set up a reel-to-reel tape recorder and microphones to supplement our practice sessions. We would rehearse obsessively for hours, breaking the tension with quiet interludes of conversation and lovemaking.

There was a kindness now that surrounded

each encounter as we came to the full realization that even the slightest gesture was no longer routine. The depth of our love and the anticipation of its ending helped to make every sight, sound, touch, and taste as exciting as the first and as emotional as the last.

As we moved into May, the campus became alive with movement as the school year drew to a close. While others vied for study seats in the libraries, Bob and I remained inside his apartment in the isolation of rehearsal. When weekends no longer afforded us adequate time, we added weekdays to our schedule as well. Singing, adapting, loving. It was a wonderful time that filled my heart with a wealth of memories.

When Georgia was home, she usually stayed in the bedroom during our living room rehearsals. Often we would ask her to come out and listen to us, and the three of us would discuss how we could improve. She had a good sense of the music and what her husband was trying to achieve. I began to realize how well these two people fit together. She was truly interested and her suggestions were always appropriate. If she had any idea of the relationship Bob and I had, she never let it show.

I had invited my family to make the journey

from Munster to Bloomington to attend our performance. In a show of unity and support, my mother, father, and brothers crowded into the Waller apartment to watch our final rehearsal the night before the event. I suffered momentary panic as I watched my mother's keen eye take everything in. But as soon as Bob and I began to sing, the mood lightened. Everything seemed perfect when my family and I left the apartment and headed out to dinner. I was on top of the world until my mom took me aside.

"I could have cried for that woman," she said. Her next words spat at me like machine-gun fire. "How could you stand before that pregnant woman with your eyes full of her husband like that?"

Up until that moment I had honestly believed that Bob and I existed only in our own private world, hurting no one. My mother was brittle, punishing, as always. I'd been numb to her condemnations of me since March. But if she could see what was going on, so could others. For the first time I was forced to look at our relationship differently, in a way that gave my mother the right to be ashamed of me.

I had no answer for her. Worse, I had no answer for myself. My only consolation was that it would all be over soon. Very soon. Sleep came hard that night as I thought about how wrong it was for me to love a man whose life belonged to another. I reassured myself that once I was gone, everything would be all right for Bob and Georgia.

The Acacia house was the farthest west in the line of sororities and fraternities that lined Third Street. It was a large, old white house with a lawn that sloped gently to the sidewalk, a lawn that had been transformed into a mini-fairground for the event. A small stage, decorated in Indiana University's colors of red and white, was placed at the far end, with rows of folding chairs lined up across the width of the lawn.

After showing my family to their seats, I joined Bob in a small room inside the fraternity house for a last-minute tuning and rehearsal. How strange it felt to be with him in a public place—away from the safety of the West University Apartments. This, coupled with my conversation with my mother and subsequent loss of sleep, compounded my growing stage fright and I began to visibly shake. Bob tried to reassure me, cajoling with gentle humor and compliments. Soon we were being ushered down the hall, across the lawn, and up the stairs to the stage and the waiting crowd.

Slowly, deliberately, I began to play, to sing. After the first few chords, I settled down as practiced skill gained control over nerves. Flashbulbs and applause decorated our performance, and when it was over we descended from the stage and were greeted by a flurry of compliments.

I was pleased if not content, and when my family left the following afternoon, I went immediately to Bob's apartment. After congratulating each other on our success the night before, we fell silent, both realizing the time to say good-bye was near. We had shared something special, something we'd remember forever, but it was coming to an end. I would be going home for the summer; he and Georgia were heading to Iowa for several weeks. Still, before we separated, I had final exams and Bob had some things to take care of.

"Georgia is going to go on ahead next week," he commented. "She wants to spend some extra time with her family before I get there." I was surprised at this news and wondered if he'd had anything to do with her decision. But I was too happy to question this remarkable gift of fate. We would be alone together for our final days.

Like anything long anticipated, long dreaded, the hours moved too quickly as our week raced by. During the mornings, I studied at his wood-slab desk while Bob went about his business. In the afternoons, as the sun edged its way across campus, we'd sit on the bedroom floor and he would sing his favorite songs into the tape recorder, creating a piece of himself that would belong only to me.

We talked of Iowa and northwest Indiana, familiarizing each other with our separate destinations. I would be returning to Munster, far away from where he would be singing as he had in the past, at a little bar on weekends.

"There's a dim light on the wall near the back of the bar. I'll always see you in its glow," he told me. We lived each passing day with all the power and passion that was promised when we met.

On our last day together, I woke him with a light tap on the door and quickly nestled in beside him on sheets warmed by his sleep. There in his bed in the early morning hours, I memorized every moment of our lovemaking, every second of my arms around his young and strong body, trying to hold the image of him and our love inside me forever. When the morning finally slipped away, Bob reluctantly left the bed and picked up his guitar instead of his clothes. He turned the tape recorder on and began to sing a new song he had written about our time together.

And freight trains will rumble and trucks will roll
Planes will always fly westward bound
'Til in springtime once again, when I find you, my
little friend,
One more hour and I'll be gone.

This song was different than any of the others, for it carried the hope that one day we might find each other again in some far-off springtime.

Finishing the song, he carefully rewound the tape, rose, and stepped into the bathroom. I heard the rush of the water as it spouted from the showerhead and hit the cool tile wall. Suddenly the sound grew louder. Turning, I saw him standing in the open doorway. Naked. Inviting me to join him.

I left the bed and moved across the room. He took my hand in his and led me into the shower. Once inside, we moved into the steam, ducking under the warmth of the falling water. He held me for a moment, the water cascading down our bodies. He took the soap and lovingly worked my back into a creamy lather, moving across my skin with care, gently pausing and massaging as he went.

We stood silently as one, molded together in a tight embrace, caressed by the gentle spray. Sad thoughts moved through my mind, never wanting the moment to end, yet knowing the end was nearer than ever.

When at last we stepped from the shower, the vulnerability of my nakedness swept over me. This was an intimacy different from sexuality and, even now, after all we had shared, my old fears came rushing back. Was this the moment when he would discover how really plain I was? He didn't seem to notice, and I let go of my old worries as I watched him shave. The sun caught the edge of the razor as he made quick work of an overnight stubble, finishing by splashing water onto his face and rubbing it down with a fresh towel.

By the time he had stepped from the bathroom, I had finished dressing and watched as he buttoned a shirt and slid into his faded jeans. The air hung damp and still. Producing a key, Bob asked if I would water the plants and keep an eye on things in the apartment for the next week while I was taking my final exams. I took the key, said I would, and felt good about the trust such responsibility implied.

We moved through the rest of the day, functioning as humans do at difficult times. Autopilot working, emotions on hold. He showed me around the kitchen and invited me to help myself to the scattering of food left behind. Next, he focused on his work area, organizing and reorganizing, until it was orderly and neat.

In the late afternoon we stretched out side by side on the living room sofa. Emotionally exhausted, this period of rest turned into our first and only gentle sleep in each other's arms. It was a kind of bonding, devoid of sexual intimacy, that united us ever more strongly. It was the last untroubled slumber I would have for quite some time to come.

The darkness woke us much later, hair matted

with perspiration, cheeks tattooed with sleep wrinkles. We carried on slowly, knowing our time together had ended. No words. No need for them. I wondered if our special telepathy would reach across the miles between Indiana and Iowa. Bob did not pack up my tape for me that night. He left it on the recorder, knowing I would need to turn to it in the days ahead. I gathered my things and joined him in the hall. One last embrace before I turned and went out the door.

I have no recollection of the beauty of Kinsey Hollow that night. My head was pounding mercilessly, the pain shooting down into my arms. Some huge formation had found its way into my throat and I couldn't swallow. When I couldn't fight any longer, the tears finally came from a place so deep within I was afraid they'd never stop.

No one saw me enter Read Center as I padded silently across the linoleum floor. The elevator was empty, my friends had retired to their rooms, and my roommate had graduated and gone. I opened the door of my room and thought again of Bob. His touch, his kindness, his songs of love. The smell of his skin, the warmth of his body. And then I crumpled onto the middle of the floor.

Mikki found me there some time later, my face and eyes swollen by my endless tears. She shook me and called out my name, but I didn't respond. She ran to get a few of our closest friends and they half carried, half dragged me into the bathroom. One of the girls filled the bathtub with cold water while others walked me around the room. When the tub was full, they brought me to the edge of it, forced me to my knees, and held my head underwater in a frantic attempt to make me fight for breath. They were successful, and I came up sputtering, my lungs heaving.

A little later, after I was back in my room, I remember someone bringing me aspirin and a glass of water. The water was soothing but the aspirin stuck in my swollen throat. Coughing between tears, I was helped to my feet and deposited in Mikki's room for the rest of the night. She sat beside me, rocking me like a small child, quietly reassuring me that everything would be okay, but even she could hear the emptiness of her words.

Some time later she went to her bed and fell asleep. There would be none of that for me. When I wasn't crying, I was fighting as hard as I could to keep from bursting out of the dorm and running back to Bob. To hold him once more, to kiss his mouth, his eyes, his hair. To feel the warmth and safety of his arms. To be once more transported to that dimension that belonged only to us. And then the tears would begin again as I realized that whatever good that might do for the moment, it would only make things harder in the long run. My mind began retracing the last five months and my pillow absorbed tears of both joy and sorrow.

I was numb by the time Mikki woke up. I was able to talk to her briefly without tears. She wanted me to go with her to the cafeteria and get something to eat, but I declined. She didn't push. Even though Bob had been gone only a few hours, I told her I had to go check on things. I held out my hand to show her his key and realized I had been clutching it all night. It was firmly imprinted into my flesh. As I stared down at it, Mikki made me promise not to leave until she could walk over with me. She dressed quickly, keeping a watchful eye on me. When she was ready I leaned on her to get up, and she put her arm around me as we walked to the elevator. A couple of friends from the night before saw us and whispered to her. She quietly thanked them for their help and said I'd be okay. The elevator doors slid open and Mikki and I were the only riders all the way to the ground floor.

The air smelled fresh and warm and my spirits lifted, reminding me of the day Bob had first kissed me. I looked straight at his building with an intensity of purpose and moved my feet deliberately on the familiar sidewalk that was once again taking me there. Mikki came into the building with me and helped me turn the key in Bob's lock. She looked at me questioningly and I opened the door wide enough for her to step inside. She came into the hallway but no further. She respected the privacy of these little rooms and stayed only long enough to be sure I was all right. I walked into the living room, breathing in the smells of him. He was gone, yet he was there. The tears came again but without the desperation. Deciding no harm would come of leaving me there, Mikki gave me a hug and went out the door, closing it behind her. I locked myself in and then began the slow process of moving alone through the apartment.

Each room had its own memories. In the living room I saw us laughing as we sat together on the floor listening to music. My leg began to feel warm in the spot where he had often placed his hand. I began talking to him, telling him all the things I hadn't been able to say the night before. Perhaps the walls would someday relay my words to him in a way only he could hear.

I noticed the plants and remembered my promise to care for them, so I went into the kitchen to find a water container. The memories grabbed hold of me again, and as I remembered the sandwiches he took such pains to make, I suddenly realized I was hungry. I found bread and salami in the refrigerator and set about duplicating the Waller sandwich. I felt as though he were at my shoulder, guiding me. That done, I grabbed a beer and went back into the living room. I sat in his study chair and looked at the titles of his books while I ate. I shook my head with wonder at this versatile man who was an authority on business management, a scholarship-winning basketball player, an accomplished musician, a singer and songwriter, an adoring husband, an expectant father, and the love of a young girl named Jana. As the sadness began to build, I glanced away from the books and, in doing so, caught sight of the plants. I picked up my plate and returned it to the kitchen. Finding a tall glass, I filled it with water and went about fulfilling my last promise to Robert.

I was beginning to feel tired. *A good sign,* I thought. But I was not yet ready to go into the bedroom. Instead, I lay alone on the couch where we had been together just hours before. As I closed my weary eyes, I wished for his arms around me and slept fitfully until darkness once again awakened me and I had to return to the dorm.

The next day I had to start preparing for my finals, so I packed up my books and took them to Bob's. I studied at his desk for hours before getting up to stretch. I walked over to the bedroom doorway. The memories rushed at me from every furnishing, from the tape recorder waiting for me on the floor, from the streaks of sunshine stretching through the window. *No, not yet,* I thought as the tears began to fall. I returned to my studies but could no longer concentrate, so I checked that the plants were still moist, then packed up my books and headed back to the dorm. I had to complete my freshman year, though I had no thought to excel; simply passing would be just fine. I avoided the distractions of the apartment long enough to get through my testing. After my last exam I headed straight to Bob's. I had been away for three days and the plants needed water. My parents were coming to pick me up in the morning. It was time for the last good-bye.

This time I didn't avoid the bedroom. I walked directly in and sat down on the floor in front of the tape recorder. Bob had left my tape threaded, so I had only to reach out and press the Play button. When I did, his voice filled the room and I felt safe and warm again. As he sang to me, I rose and walked around the room, caressing each piece of furniture as though it were a part of him. I stood in the tiny bathroom staring into the mirror, hoping to see his reflection. I noticed he had made the bed. It was the first time I had seen it made up in a long time. I walked over to it and ran my hand across the covers. Without mussing his work, I extracted his pillow and, as I held it to me, noticed it still carried the scent of him. I laid down on the floor holding the pillow and listening to him sing. The tears trickled from the outside corners of my eyes, but I was smiling. I had loved and had been loved. The thought of whether it would ever happen again didn't cross my mind.

As it grew dark, I decided it was time to take care of business. Replacing the pillow carefully, I smoothed and patted the bed until it looked exactly as I had found it. With the tape on its seventh run-through, I turned on a few lights and went into the kitchen to wash the knife and plate I'd left in the sink earlier. I set them aside while I filled the tall glass with water one last time and went to the living room to tend to the plants. I glanced around the room and made sure everything was in its place. Returning to the kitchen, I dried the dishes and put them away. I wiped the countertop, shook out and folded the towel, and turned off the light. I went back into the bedroom and waited for the last song to play before rewinding the tape, then removed it from the spindle and placed it carefully in its box. With one last survey of our bedroom world, I turned off the light switch. Now the only illumination came from the light in the small hallway. Hugging my tape box, I lingered in the hallway for one last look around. Then, leaving the key on the end table, I turned my back to the apartment and moved slowly toward the door. I thought of taking one more backward glance, but instead I put the knob in the lock position and stepped into the outer hallway, closing the door behind me for the last time.

SIX

Separate Ways

Gone are the days when you and I would lay together
Oh, how the times would roll!
But soon, much too soon summertime had come
And bound separate ways were we . . .

Summer 1967
Munster, Indiana

Morning arrived early, my emotions shaking me awake long before my alarm clock sprang to life at 7 A.M. My parents would be showing up around noon and I wanted to be completely packed when they arrived. The northwest corner of Indiana operates on Central time, while the rest of the state, Bloomington included, is on Eastern time. My mother and father would have left home at 5 A.M. to make the six-hour drive and, since they'd be facing the return trip as well, I thought the least I could do was to be ready and waiting.

Dragging my suitcases out from under the bed, I moved around the room in a mindless ritual, aching out of emotional instinct, no longer needing to think of Bob to generate the hurt our separation caused. The clothes on the closet shelf were folded, ready to be transferred into one suitcase; the contents of three dresser drawers fit neatly into the other suitcase. A huge garment bag accommodated the hanging items and there was room in the bottom for shoes. Reference books, school supplies, and toiletries went into boxes along with my now-silent alarm clock. Finally I stripped my bed, placed the folded linens into pillowcases, and lined everything with precision out in the hall.

The entire dormitory was closing down, its walls saying a silent good-bye as I went into Mikki's room to help my friend get organized. She was rushing around in a panic, tossing things toward a suitcase in the middle of the room. Her boyfriend had just arrived and she was far from ready. I knelt down next to her suitcase, folding and repacking, while he politely took my suitcases and boxes to the lobby.

Our teamwork played neatly into the game of rush, pack, run, and before I could get used to the idea, Mikki's room was empty and she was ready to go. We stood quietly looking at each other for a moment, silently recalling events shared over the year, and then dissolved into a tight embrace.

"Thank you, my friend," I said. "Thank you so very much for everything." She hugged tighter in response as we both fought back tears.

Finally forcing myself to turn away, flashing a shaky smile, I bent to pick up my purse and oversized book bag, which held the precious tape recording. Arm in arm, we moved downstairs together. Out in front of Read Center, Mikki's boyfriend was waiting, engine running, passenger door open.

"You take care of yourself," she whispered, giving me one last hug. Bending to get into the car, she called back, "And be sure to write to me." Then she was gone. I turned and walked over to my suitcases, all lined up on the sidewalk, when I heard a horn honking. My parents had arrived.

Though my family wasn't perfect, I was glad to see them. As my dad and I loaded my luggage into the back of the station wagon, the familiarity helped to fill a growing void. Physically, I was leaving Bloomington but, unknown to them, a part of me would stay behind.

To give my parents a chance to stretch and unwind, we pulled the car into a parking space and walked over to the Student Union for lunch. The lawn that fronted the Delta Gamma house was now lush and manicured. The woods were in bloom, allowing only trickles of sunlight to filter through the dense foliage as we approached the pedestrian bridge. Bouncing and swirling over the small, smooth rocks that formed its bed, the brook provided a natural birdbath for a bright red cardinal. He preened and picked, then flapped his wings in enthusiastic splendor. Life was regenerated everywhere but in my heart.

Arriving at the alumni restaurant in the Union, we ordered and enjoyed far better food than the standard cafeteria fare I was used to. As I ate, my father shared the good news that he had arranged a summer job for me at the steel mill where he worked. The pay was far better than most college students would earn waiting tables or selling clothes, and I looked forward to the opportunity to earn some cash.

When it came time to leave the campus, I volunteered to take the first shift behind the wheel. On the way out of town, I took Third Street so I could show my parents the Alpha Xi Delta house I would be returning to in the fall. I'd have preferred staying in the dorm and rooming with Mikki, but pledged the sorority in hopes of pleasing my mother. It wasn't the house of her choice, so my effort generated little excitement. *Oh, well,* I thought, with the same attitude I'd had since March. *At least I tried.*

Out on the highway, with the radio playing, conversation was minimal. My parents were tired and I was remembering Bob's white skin. How strange, after all the years of despising my own pale skin, that I would find his so beautiful. As the billboards and mile markers flew by, my mind began playing his songs about highways in the rain, shutting out whatever tunes were coming from the car radio. Somewhere along the way, my dad took over the wheel, and by the time we pulled into our driveway, it was close to dark. Nevertheless, I could see our house perfectly nestled in the quiet suburban neighborhood of well-tended lawns and small trees. It was a simple, one-story home. Grayish-tan brick and picture windows formed one of the front corners; a flower box of matching brick sat below the windows. My brothers appeared at the front door, as did our dog, an aging, fawn-colored boxer named Taffy. She was delighted to see me, her stubby little tail batting rapidly back and forth. I gave her a giant hug as the boys unloaded my suitcases from the car. They were teenagers now and not given to displays of affection these days, so I just walked alongside them as we went into the house.

Over the next week I looked up old friends, went to the beach, and made a couple of trips to a special restaurant where I had eaten every day during high school. It was called Maid-Rite's and the fare was crumbled hamburger cooked by steam.

My few short days of leisure dissolved quickly as my summer job approached, and soon I was trading in my swimsuit for the standard steel-mill issue of metatarsal shoes, safety glasses, and hard hat. On Monday I reported to the 76-inch Hot Strip Mill shipping office in Plant 2, far away from dusty roads, winding rivers, and fields of wheat blown by summer wind.

The office was located on a concrete island, surrounded by racks of huge sheets of steel. Overhead cranes with giant magnets swinging on thick cables soared above me, sirens screaming, in constant action. Inside the office I met my supervisor, set apart in his glass-enclosed office, and was shown my summer duties, which involved keeping records of the shipping operations. Simple and redundant, the work provided a nice diversion from my constant thoughts of Bob. Still, he drifted in and out of my head. Upon leaving the mill that first day, I noticed I could see a touch of Lake Michigan from the loading dock. In the midst of wailing sirens and crashing steel, I felt a momentary peacefulness and decided this would be my place to remember him.

When I returned home that evening, I found a letter from Bob sitting on my bed. Obviously my mother had put it there and, because his name and address appeared on the envelope, she knew who it was from. I was uncomfortable with the thought, too uncomfortable to even read the letter in my room. I needed a special place to separate my life with him from the reality around me. Tucking the letter inside my shirt, I headed for the basement and the solitude it offered. On my way through the kitchen, I passed my mother, who raised an eyebrow questioningly.

"Look, Mom," I said, "I understand and agree with what you said in Bloomington. But I see nothing wrong with continuing to be friends with Bob and, I assure you, that's all there is to it now." Before she could say anything, I turned and disappeared down the stairs. Faithful Taffy roused herself from a nap in the back hall to follow me.

My father had built a workroom for himself in one section of the basement and another part was set up as a den with a kitchenette. Some unused space remained in the back corner and I spent the rest of the day fashioning a small cubicle for myself there. A slab of wood from the workroom laid across some stacked bricks formed a desk; a folding chair dragged out of storage provided a place to sit. An ugly old privacy screen painted white with green flowers served to close off the area. A candle for mood and a cigarette for sanity completed my sanctuary. I patted Taffy, who sat down beside me, and slowly, deliberately, I opened the letter and returned to Bob's world.

He was still in Iowa, playing his guitar in the little bar he had described to me, the tiny light glowing on the back wall. He spoke of the restraint it took for him not to throw open his apartment door and come after me the night we parted. The hardest thing he had ever done, and probably ever would do, he said. Silent tears welled, then flowed down my cheeks as I remembered that night.

He hoped all was well with me and gave the date he would be back in Bloomington. There was even mention that I'd be welcome to come down for a visit in midsummer, if I cared to.

I reread the letter several times before folding it in half and taking out my cigarette lighter. I lit the lower corner of the letter and watched as the flame spread through his words, voiding them to the eyes of anyone other than me. I was determined to keep our feelings private and known to us alone. Destroying the letter was part of that. Soon there was nothing left but ashes and the memory of the only emotional letter I would ever receive from him.

My days at the Hot Strip passed pretty quickly. In the evenings Taffy and I would retreat to my cubicle and I would play the songs Bob had written for me, holding my guitar as close as I had held him. Without access to a tape machine, I had no way to listen to him, so this was the only way for me to hear the music. I began wondering if I would ever hear his voice sing the words again and decided to write them down. The next weekend I added a pad of paper to the standard contents of my beach bag and went out to the Indiana Dunes to record the gentle words from his heart. After returning home I tucked the pages into a nondescript folder that held all my handwritten words for a multitude of songs so they wouldn't attract any special attention.

When the day of Bob's return to Bloomington arrived, I gathered stationery with matching envelopes and several pens before going downstairs to my private desk. I lit the candle and a cigarette and began to write. Not wanting to upset him, I didn't mention my hysteria on the night we parted but admitted I, too, had fought the impulse to return to him. I described the steel mill and the details of my job, accenting the view of Lake Michigan. I told him whenever I thought of him—which was often—I could no longer hear the sirens or crashing steel, only the peace that his image never failed to bring.

I ended by saying I'd love to visit but would have to look into whether I could get time off. I signed my letter as he had signed his, "Ride Easy," then sealed it in an envelope. The next day I bought a stamp and sent the letter out through the plant mail to avoid involving my mother in the process.

The days moved more slowly as I awaited a reply. I kept to myself, rebuffed overtures from the office flirt, and returned home nightly to spend the evening with my dog in my basement cubicle.

At last another letter arrived. Having learned of my summer job, Bob now suggested I come to Bloomington over a weekend. That wouldn't require any time away from work and I thought the idea sounded great. Surprisingly I was able to get permission from my mother. I didn't know whether she realized this was a necessary experience or whether she was just tired of struggling with me. I picked a weekend, called for train schedules, and wrote to Bob with the details. He replied with a note saying he'd be at the train station when I arrived.

As I awaited the appointed day, I composed a song for him in my best high school French. It told of a young girl wandering through life alone, searching for a lost friend. I wrote it in French because one of the songs Bob particularly liked was a ballad about a French girl. And, I must confess, I was so awed by his talent with words, I didn't want to risk putting something together for him that would be inferior to what he had written for me. I gave it a haunting tune and found myself humming it on the train to drown out the nervous pounding of my heart when the day finally arrived and I found myself speeding toward Bloomington.

My thoughts bounced along in time with the clattering rails as I wondered what it would be like to see him again. I knew it would be different; after all, our affair was over. But I hadn't stopped caring and I wondered if I'd be able to make the transition from lover to friend. It seemed like a lifetime had gone by since May and I missed him terribly.

What is he thinking? I silently asked myself. *What is he feeling?*

Before I had a chance to think through my

feelings, the train was pulling into the station. I was both excited and anxious as I momentarily remained in my seat, trying to collect myself. I looked out the window into the midafternoon sun and scanned the platform. I didn't see him anywhere. Good. *He's running late,* I thought. This would give me a chance to figure out what I should say, how I should act. I collected my bag and guitar case from the overhead rack and stepped from the train behind the other passengers. I wasn't prepared to find Bob standing right in front of me.

"Hi," I said, obviously surprised.

"Hi," he replied politely, taking my guitar case to lighten my load. "How was the trip?"

There was no hug, no kiss, not even an arm around my shoulder. My senses were instantly dulled by his lack of emotion and I answered in a very matter-of-fact tone as I walked alongside him to his car, a beige Volkswagen Beetle. It occurred to me I'd never known what kind of car he drove. He opened the passenger door for me. I tossed my bag into the back and climbed in. Then he walked around to the driver's side and carefully laid my guitar on the backseat before getting in beside me and starting the car.

Like two strangers, we made small talk as I

watched his right hand move the gearshift instead of reaching out to hold mine. Even though I realized that I hadn't thought this visit out very carefully, no amount of time would have prepared me for this restraint, this by-the-numbers exchange.

My God, it's really over, I thought to myself. The full meaning of our agreement began to hit me. But how was I to turn off my feelings? I watched as he demonstrated how it was done. So this was why he'd wanted me to come. Once again he was teaching me. And the lesson was far from over. We parked in front of the apartment building and went inside. Georgia was waiting for us, gracious as always, wearing her pregnancy beautifully. Instead of retreating to the bedroom or going off to work, she sat down and talked, welcoming me like an old friend. As we spoke, I realized again how much I genuinely liked this lady. Seeing them together brought back memories of what Bob had said: "She fits me like an old shoe, comfortable, dependable." He was right. Georgia was perfect for him. I was a city girl who would never be truly happy trading bright lights for dusty roads.

We enjoyed an early dinner and then Georgia excused herself. She tired easily these days, she said with a smile. Bob and I got out our guitars and began, once again, to play and sing together softly. A while later he checked on her and found her sleeping. Returning to the living room, he sat down on the couch and patted the cushion next to him, inviting me to come over and sit beside him. At long last he took my hand, leaned over, and kissed me. It was a gentle kiss of caring and understanding, lacking the passion of the ones we had previously shared, but nice just the same. I looked into his face and saw the love was still there, and that was enough for me. Over the next hour I sang my French song for him and saw tears form in his eyes.

"I worry about you, Jana," he said. "What's to become of you?" He wanted me to find a life of my own with someone and live happily. I promised him I would, still not understanding how difficult that was going to be.

He put sheets on the couch for me and produced a pillow for my head before giving me a hug and saying good night. Then he was gone. I lay awake for some time, reviewing the day, looking deep inside my feelings. I loved Bob more then than I did at any other time in our relationship. Perhaps that's why I fell asleep pledging to set him free. I resolved that I would try to start dating, leap back into the game of dinners on your best behavior, movies followed by good-night kisses.

The following morning I worked at being brave and emotionless as Bob drove me to the train station. I promised to call as soon as I arrived back on campus in September and waved a silent good-bye from my window seat. Not until the station was out of sight did I allow my tears to fall.

SEVEN

Love Everlasting
Always True

You know that I can make you no promises
Of love everlasting always true
But when I sing of rivers and the highways in the rain
My thoughts will drift always back to you.

September 1967
Bloomington, Indiana

By the end of summer, I was more than ready to return to Bloomington, eager to be independent once more. I moved into the sorority but not into the sorority-girl routine. Rather than blend in, I separated myself, opting for one of two single rooms tucked into a corner on the second floor. A girl from California was housed in the other and, while we became friends, I cherished my privacy.

My little corner included a small bed, a

dresser, and a clothes pole. A tiny window was positioned high on one wall and under it sat a desk and chair. I also had my own telephone and I quickly used it to call Bob.

He sounded happy to hear from me and I found myself surprisingly comfortable in the role of old friend, though the sound of his voice still tugged at my heart. The summer visit had been good for me. I listened happily as he told me he had begun performing with a banjo player named Wayne at the Holiday Inn out on Highway 37.

"Would you like to come hear us?" he asked.

"I'd love to," I answered, and we made plans for him to pick me up at the sorority house on Saturday night.

My next call was to Mikki, who had returned to dorm life and was anxious to see my little room. We met early the next day, delighted to be together again. Even though we'd exchanged letters over the summer, we found plenty to talk about. She was glad to hear I was adjusting to the new relationship with Bob, and discussing it with her made me even stronger.

We moved furniture around in each other's rooms and then went shopping for knickknacks.

She was my guest for lunch at the sorority house, and we went for pizza together at dinner. She was my friend, my confidante, and much more of a sister to me than any sorority girl would ever be.

Bob called Saturday afternoon to confirm our plans and picked me up right on time. He looked wonderful as he stood beside the now familiar Volkswagen, holding the door for me. I wanted to give him a friendly hug but resisted the impulse, afraid it might confuse things.

Once we arrived I helped him carry his equipment into the lobby. Because I was only eighteen, though, the manager would not allow me into the bar area, where Bob and Wayne would be playing. This did not sit well with my former lover, who argued to no avail. In the end we found a small table for me in the restaurant adjacent to the bar. A swinging door would separate us, but I would be able to hear everything. Bob was visibly upset as he seated me and promised he would come and sit with me during breaks. I was to order anything I wanted; it would go on his tab. Reluctantly he disappeared into the bar.

At first I felt self-conscious about sitting there

by myself, but when he began to play and I heard the familiar sound of the voice I loved, I felt only loneliness. Despite his visits between sets, I couldn't shake the feeling. He took me back to the sorority house during a long break later in the evening, because I still had a curfew. I was glad to get away from the discomfort I felt at the Holiday Inn and barely heard him promise to call the next day.

I wanted nothing more than to be alone, and my little room at the sorority provided the perfect hiding place. I ran up the stairs, speaking to no one, and shut the door tightly behind me. I struggled with the old, painted window frame, finally opening it, then I collapsed onto my bed. I still felt the heat of my embarrassment and I needed to breathe the cool night breeze. I stared up at the sky but didn't notice any stars. For the first time I was angry. Because of the mandates of society, I had to let go of the man I loved and I didn't need any more of its rules to come along and remind me of where I stood. Silent tears burned my eyes as I began to cry for all the days gone by and all the lonely nights that lay ahead.

Bob called the next day. As if he were reading

my thoughts, he spoke gently to me, like he did in the early days. He thought I should have been permitted in the bar area as long as I didn't order any alcoholic drinks.

"I guess there must be a different policy governing entertainers," he said. "If I'd had any idea you were going to have to sit out in the restaurant, I'd never have dragged you out there."

"You didn't drag me," I protested, not wanting him to feel bad. "I wanted to hear you sing and I did. It was fine, really."

Despite my words, I think he knew how left out I felt because he invited me to come over and practice with him and Wayne later in the week. Though nothing could change the situation, I appreciated what he was trying to do, and his invitation helped perk up my spirits. I told him I'd be there.

Classes began on Monday morning and soon the routine of college life was back in full swing. For me, that included a trip to Bob's a few days later. Wayne was already there and I could hear the music from down the hallway. Bob opened the door after I knocked and Wayne acknowledged my arrival by playing a quick run on his banjo as I entered and sat down. He was a gangly young man with horn-rimmed glasses, but what he lacked in looks was more than compensated for by his personality. He wore a constant, engaging smile, was bright of mind as well as wit, and I knew I liked him from the minute I'd met him at the Holiday Inn. We hadn't had much of a chance to get acquainted that night, so it was fun getting to know him in the relaxed atmosphere of the apartment.

Although I'd heard how well his instrument blended with Bob's style and delivery, I'd never seen anyone play the banjo before. It was amazing to watch his fingers fly up and down the long, ebony neck of the instrument. I was even more impressed when I discovered how heavy it was. Unlike guitars that are made of wood and relatively lightweight, his five-string banjo was made of solid metal with vellum stretched tautly across the body. I couldn't imagine holding it for any period of time, let alone maintaining the feather-light touch required to play it properly.

Wayne stayed with us for a couple of hours and then departed, leaving Bob and me alone in the apartment. Though she was no longer working, Georgia was out and Bob said she wouldn't be back until early evening. I assumed the idea of three musicians picking their way through the afternoon had driven her to seek more peaceful surroundings.

I looked up and found Bob's eyes staring at me in the old, still familiar way. In spite of our agreement and all our good intentions, the temptation was irresistible and we found ourselves once again in each other's arms. Over the summer we had both come to realize that going our separate ways was far more difficult than we'd imagined and we were grateful for this brief respite from our plight. We had already been apart for a longer period of time than we had been together but, instead of experiencing the kind of passion that might be expected under these circumstances, we approached each other in a quiet way.

As wonderful as it was to be close again, we were both resigned to our situation and weary from our efforts to keep our pledge to each other. We made love with slow and easy familiarity. Each touch was an act of healing, each moment an unexpected gift. Our story was over; this tryst was no more than an afterthought. It was a means of letting go, not holding on. No new hope was born, no promises amended. We separated with a kiss that day that said, "I'll remember you," and nothing more.

When I returned on Saturday to resume the regular schedule we'd had in the spring, the routine was a bit different. This time his wife answered the door and invited me in. The three of us talked a bit and I marveled at how wonderful she looked. She laughed and said something about how deceiving appearances can be, then went into the bedroom and shut the door. She was going to read or watch TV while we played our guitars.

By this time I had learned enough to be able to help Bob warm up before his performance onstage at the Holiday Inn. We laughed as he did some voice exercises and then we went over a few songs. Regardless of whatever else was going on with us, we always had the music as the one constant in our lives. It had brought us together, added depth to our love, and softened our sorrow. Together or apart, it would always be there for us.

Time passed quickly and soon Bob needed to shower and dress. While I packed up, we talked again about the situation at the bar and concluded there was no point in my coming out there again.

"What would you think about staying here with Georgia on Saturday nights?" he asked. "The baby's due in about a month and I get pretty nervous about leaving her alone for long periods of time. I mentioned it to her and she thought it was a nifty idea—that is, unless you have other plans. . . ."

I smiled and shook my head as his voice trailed off. He smiled back, knowing I wasn't dating anyone but too thoughtful to take the liberty of making the assumption.

"You could bring your books over and study," he continued, "or just listen to music, help yourself to beer or anything else you'd like. If something happens, you'd be here to call me right away."

I didn't pause for a second before agreeing to help, although I wasn't sure what I'd need to do to get around curfew. Now that I was in a house instead of the dorm, I knew it was possible to sign out for an entire night but didn't know the policy on being late.

"I might need a note from you explaining

what I'm doing," I told him. "Let me find out and I'll call you in the morning."

That was fine with him. He was happy to do whatever was necessary, including offering me the living room couch again if our only option was for me to sign out.

My enthusiasm was genuine when I spoke to our housemother that evening. She had seen me come and go with my guitar, so she was not surprised when I began by telling her about my lessons. Briefly I explained Bob's request and told her I would like to do something to help my teacher and his wife. A widow with grown children of her own, she was quick to understand. Yes, there was a procedure for coming in after curfew. There was an after-hours buzzer located at the outside door of her ground-floor apartment. She told me it was primarily used by girls who violated curfew and she hated having to give the standard late-night lecture. "It would be a welcome change," she said, "to help you out." Practiced in her motherly role, she cautioned me to "be sure to have Bob drive you home."

When I called with the news the next day, Bob was delighted and asked me to express his appreciation to my housemother. Of course, he would drive me home and see that I got inside safely. I also was to tell her it would only be for a few weeks, as the baby was due in October.

I arrived the following Saturday night with an armful of books instead of my guitar. Bob smelled of soap and shampoo when he answered the door, a tie draped around his shirt collar. He had cleared off his desk to make room for me and I put my books down as Georgia came out of the bedroom, nearly colliding with her husband as he rushed around gathering up his jacket and guitar case. He leaned over and kissed her good-bye and then was out the door, leaving us laughing behind him.

Georgia asked if I wanted to get started on my studies right away or, if not, maybe I'd like to see some of the baby gifts they'd received. It was no contest, I told her, as I followed her into the bedroom. The big lamp was on, making the room bright and cheerful, and it was as though I was seeing it for the first time. It was completely different from the romantic room Bob and I had shared. Gift boxes decorated the table and dresser top, and a small crib now occupied the space in the middle of the floor where Bob and I used to sit and sing.

As she began showing me the contents of the boxes, Georgia's eyes sparkled and her voice took on an added gentleness. I was touched by how carefully she handled the tiny clothes, folding and patting them as she returned them to their boxes. It must have taken an hour for us to go through every single item. I was disappointed when we finished and I had no further excuse for avoiding my books. Georgia said that she would be watching TV and working on a sweater she was knitting for the baby, and that I was welcome to take a break and join her whenever I wanted. I went out to Bob's desk and opened a book but found it difficult to concentrate. My mind whirled with thoughts of the day when I would have a husband like Bob and a child on the way. Would it ever come? Would I ever know love like Georgia did?

The phone startled me when it rang. I was surprised to see it sitting on the desk. I'd never noticed it before. In all the times I'd been to the apartment, no one had ever called. Georgia asked me if I could answer it. It would probably be Bob. She was right. He was on a break and wondered how things were going.

"Just fine," I told him. "We've been doing girl stuff, looking at all the adorable baby clothes."

He laughed with understanding and maybe a little relief.

"Georgia's doing great," I reassured him as I caught sight of her emerging from the bedroom out of the corner of my eye. "In fact, here she is now."

I handed the phone over to her and then went out to the kitchen to get a beer, allowing them to have a private conversation. When I came back into the living room, Georgia handed the phone back to me and Bob gave me the phone number for the direct line to the bar.

After his call I managed to get some studying done and later went into the bedroom to check on Georgia. She was enjoying a comedy show and I sat down to watch it with her for a few minutes. From my position on the floor, I glanced back to look at her from time to time as we laughed and made comments about the program.

She was sitting in the chair between the bed

and the dresser with her bare feet propped up on a small padded stool. Her long, dark hair was pulled back and wrapped behind her head, shining under the light of the lamp at her shoulder. She wore a bra top and shorts in a bright white color that emphasized her deep summer tan. With a knitting needle in each hand, she methodically worked row after row of yarn and, as the sweater began taking shape, it covered more and more of her belly and the baby she carried. For years I would remember this image. She was truly the epitome of womanhood and I was completely in awe of her.

When the show ended, Georgia folded her knitting and stifled a yawn. I asked if she needed anything before I went back to my books, but she said she was fine. She was feeling a bit tired, though, and thought she might close her eyes for a little while. I went back out to the living room, closing the bedroom door behind me so I wouldn't disturb her. I turned the stereo on low and returned to the desk.

Bob came home right after midnight and I leaned around the bookcase as I heard him come in the door. I put my finger against my lips, signaling him to be quiet, and pointed to the bedroom door.

"I think she's fallen asleep," I whispered. "She tried to fight it, but she was really tired."

He nodded as he put down his guitar case. I gathered my books while he went into the bedroom to check on his wife. The bright light was still on, so he turned it off as he came out of the room. We left the apartment silently.

It was only about a two-minute drive to my sorority house, so Bob was brief in his recap of the evening. Some guy in the back of the bar had too much to drink and heckled the daylights out of Bob and Wayne toward the end, but for the most part it had been a pretty good show. He reached over and patted my knee as we pulled up to the sorority house, thanking me for "baby-sitting." I told him I had sincerely enjoyed it and was looking forward to doing it again.

I hopped out of the Volkswagen, books in hand, and ran up to the side door. When the housemother opened it, I turned and waved to Bob and she did, too. He smiled, put the car in gear, and drove away, returning the gesture. On

161

impulse I reached out and hugged this nice lady with my free arm. I tiptoed up to my room and got ready for bed. I felt good about what I was doing and easily settled down to a contented sleep.

The next few weeks went very much the same. Then, one crisp autumn day in October, the phone rang in my room.

"We have a baby daughter," came a voice choked with emotion. I knew he was crying and tears of my own began running down my face.

Within minutes Bob gave me a perfect mental picture of Rachael Elizabeth Waller, created from a palette of loving words. He had already written a song for her and recited it for me right then and there, though I'd soon read it myself on my copy of her birth announcement.

"Would you like to come see her?" he asked.

"Of course I would," I said. "When?"

"I'll pick you up this evening toward the end of regular visiting hours."

I almost felt like a proud parent myself as I ran downstairs to tell the housemother about Rachael. For some crazy reason I couldn't stop crying. Over the past weeks several of my sorority sisters had learned how and where I was spending my Saturday nights, so I shared the news with them on the staircase. My excitement was contagious and soon everyone was hugging everyone as word spread throughout the house. Not one of these girls had the slightest clue about the depth of my feelings about this child, but their reaction couldn't have been better. I heard later that many thought I was somehow related to the family. Maybe I was.

I didn't say a word in the car on the way to Bloomington Hospital. Bob talked the entire time and continued chattering in the parking lot, in the elevator, and all the way down the hall of the maternity ward. Then, suddenly, he was completely speechless as we stood looking through the window at his daughter. All he could do now was smile. Little Rachael was lying on her back, wriggling her tiny fingers, scrunching up her face, and kicking her legs in the confining little hospital gown. She was as beautiful as he had described, with dark hair like her mother's. She turned her head and, for the first time, I saw a red, open sore on her forehead. Although Bob had mentioned it briefly, I was not prepared for something that looked so painful. It was larger than I had expected, though smaller than a dime, but I quietly worried about whether she could feel it and if it hurt her. As if sensing my thoughts, Bob pointed out the spot and told me again that it was nothing to be concerned about. The doctor didn't seem to know what had caused it, but after checking Rachael thoroughly, he had pronounced her perfectly healthy.

I stayed at the window while Bob went into Georgia's room. The baby turned her head again with no sign of pain. I felt a little better and beamed a smile at her. She opened her tiny mouth into a yawn and slowly lowered her eyelids. Soon she was asleep.

I was in love with her, with this tiny bundle of life. I was overwhelmed. A part of me wanted to stay and watch her all night; the other part wanted to get out of that hospital as quickly as possible. I heard my name being called from down the hallway.

Turning, I saw Bob motioning to me from the door of Georgia's room. *No*, I thought. *You can't be suggesting I go in there.* Despite our friendship, I felt uncomfortable and invasive about seeing his wife on this very special day. Yet I realized that she knew I was there and would wonder why I didn't at least say hello. I moved slowly.

"Do you want to say hi to Rachael's mother?" he asked, loudly enough for her to hear.

"Sure," came the response with more enthusiasm than I felt.

I entered the doorway but went no farther. There were other people and a nurse in the room, but Georgia turned toward me and smiled. I smiled back and gave her a little wave. "Your daughter is beautiful," I mouthed. She nodded a thank-you and turned back to the others. "I'll be there in a minute," Bob said to me as I started back down the hall.

He was less talkative as we left the hospital. In the car we barely spoke. This was the last note, of the last song, of the last set, of the last performance, and we both knew it.

"Do you want to come over for a little while?" he asked.

"Well, sure," I responded, unable to conceive of turning down a request from him. "If you want me to."

It wasn't until I had a husband of my own who had to leave me and our newborn daughter at the hospital that I realized how hard it was for a man to go through his first night of fatherhood alone. A woman subconsciously prepares for the birth of her first child from the day of conception. A man, however, generally avoids the concept altogether. And even when a happily married couple learns that a baby is on the way, they each experience it very differently. A woman is fully aware of the growing child inside her and spends months getting ready to hold her baby in her arms. A man certainly notices his wife's abdomen and breasts swelling, sees and feels the baby kicking, sometimes even hears the heartbeat. But the fact remains that he is, literally, on the outside. No matter how involved he may be in the process, the full impact of having a baby really does not hit a man until he sees it, with all its parts put together, for the first time.

Bob was a unique man but he was no different from any other new father. He wanted to shout, sing, cry, and collapse all at the same time. Most of all, he wanted to be held. His wife would have been there for him if doctors and hospitals gave half a moment's thought to fathers. Their concern is only for the mother and child. Bob had to go home alone. Or, in this case, he was with me. His old friend. His old love.

He reached out to me as soon as we got inside the apartment and we held each other tight. The emotional level could not have been measured by any scale on Earth. Almost before we realized it, our clothes lay on the bedroom floor and we stood in a naked embrace beside the bed. But as the realization struck, I began to cry. Bob sat down on the edge of the bed and, taking my hands in his, he pulled me closer. When he looked up at me, I could see that he, too, was struggling to hold back tears.

"We can't do this anymore," I whispered.

He merely nodded, let go of my hands, and wrapped his arms around my hips as I reached out and hugged his head to my breast. We stayed like that for some time. Then, without a word, we released each other and picked up our clothes, dressing in silence.

It was not very late and I wanted to walk the four blocks to the sorority house, alone in the night air with my thoughts. Bob wouldn't hear of it and insisted on driving me home. When we reached the sorority house, I turned to him and smiled.

"Good night, my friend," I said, getting out of the car.

Good night and good-bye, I thought as I walked away, not looking back.

And the April rains are the coldest rains
I walk through them now with my head bent down
For lovers we were, but fools we are
For walking and living alone.

EIGHT

I Remember You

So I'll be up and on my way
I'll kiss you soft and touch your hair
And when you are grown with a love of your own
In the April mornings I'll be there.

September 1995
Los Angeles, California

Although we spoke occasionally on the phone, I saw Bob only once after the birth of his daughter. I found a new group of friends and spent all my free time with them in an apartment they shared on the south side of Bloomington. They were living commune style, as many so-called hippies did in those days, and having me hang around and play my guitar suited their lifestyle perfectly. They particularly liked Bob's songs, which I sang with great regularity while we all sat in the smoke-filled living room drinking cheap Paisano wine. At their bidding I invited Bob to come out one evening to play for us.

For Bob and me, it was a night of establishing distance. He didn't think much of my friends and was openly disapproving of a young man who hovered around me, trying to win my affection. His music was well received but, when I walked him to the door, he stopped on the steps, his face serious under the porch light.

"Be careful, Jana," he said in a somber tone before turning and walking away into the night.

Unfortunately, I was unable to grasp his warning at the time. I continued to focus on my newfound friends and, when I left Bloomington that January, I proceeded to plunge headlong into a collision course with life. But that is another story, for another time. My memories of him remained with me throughout the years.

In the spring of 1986, a verse from his song "Gentle Afternoons" proved prophetic.

So I'll be up and on my way
I'll kiss you soft and touch your hair

And when you are grown with a love of your own
In the April mornings I'll be there.

I was married with a baby daughter, living in a suburb of Toledo, Ohio, going about my nightly duties of picking up toys in the den when the voice of a newscaster reached out from the television set.

". . . in Cedar Falls, Iowa," was all I heard.

Cedar Falls? The town sounded familiar. Wasn't that where Bob said he would settle down?

On impulse I went to the phone and dialed information. The operator did, indeed, have a listing for a Robert Waller in Cedar Falls, Iowa. I wrote the number down and began wondering what it would be like to talk with him again. I found myself wanting very much to know how he was after all this time.

Early the following evening I dialed Bob's number. My hands were shaking as I held the phone to my ear, and I almost abandoned the idea. The line echoed and clicked while my thoughts raced back eighteen years. The sound of Bob's voice brought me back to the present.

"Hello?" he said.

173

"Is this Dr. Robert Waller?" I asked, as though I were bearing weighty news.

"Yes," he responded warily.

"Is this the same Robert Waller who once wrote a song about a girl named Jana?" I continued, a hint of mischief in my voice.

"Yes, it is," he laughed, his voice more relaxed. "Is this Jana?"

I wasn't surprised that he knew it was me. He sounded well and happy and we caught up as best we could in ten minutes' time. When I suggested we exchange Christmas cards during the holiday season, he thought it was a fine idea and gave me his address.

So began the correspondence that reintroduced me to my old friend. That is, until I received *The Bridges of Madison County* in the winter of 1992. I wrote Bob to thank him for sending the book and to congratulate him on his success. I never heard from him again.